How to Use the CD-ROM

System Requirements

Windows PC

- 486 or Pentium processor–based personal computer
- Microsoft Windows 95 or Windows NT 3.51 or later
- Minimum RAM: 8 MB for Windows 95 and NT
- Available space on hard disk: 8 MB Windows 95 and NT
- 2X speed CD-ROM drive or faster
- Netscape 3.0 or higher browser or MS Internet Explorer 3.0 or higher

Macintosh

- Macintosh with a 68020 or higher processor or Power Macintosh
- Apple OS version 7.0 or later
- Minimum RAM: 12 MB for Macintosh
- Available space on hard disk: 6MB Macintosh
- 2X speed CD-ROM drive or faster
- Netscape 3.0 or higher browser or MS Internet Explorer 3.0 or higher

NOTE: This CD requires Netscape 3.0 or MS Internet Explorer 3.0 or higher. You can download these products using the links on the CD-ROM Help Page.

Getting Started

Insert the CD-ROM into your drive. The CD-ROM will usually launch automatically. If it does not, click on the CD-ROM drive on your computer to launch. You will see an opening page. You can click on this page or wait for it to fade to the Copyright Page. After you click to agree to the terms of the Copyright Page, the Home Page will appear.

Moving Around

Use the buttons at the left of each screen or the underlined text at the bottom of each screen to move among the menu pages. To view a document listed on one of the menu pages, simply click on the name of the document. To quit a document at any time, click the box at the upper right-hand corner of the screen.

Use the scrollbar at the right of the screen to scroll up and down each page.

To quit the CD-ROM, you can click the Quit option at the bottom of each menu page, hit Control-Q, or click the box at the upper right-hand corner of the screen.

To Download Documents

Open the document you wish to download. Under the File pulldown menu, choose Save As. Save the document onto your hard drive with a different name. It is important to use a different name, otherwise the document may remain a read-only file.

You can also click on your CD drive in Windows Explorer and select a document to copy it to your hard drive and rename it.

In Case of Trouble

If you experience difficulty using the *Assessments A to Z* CD-ROM, please follow these steps:

1. Make sure your hardware and systems configurations conform to the systems requirements noted under "Systems Requirements" above.
2. Review the installation procedure for your type of hardware and operating system. It is possible to reinstall the software if necessary.
3. You may call Jossey-Bass/Pfeiffer Customer Service at (415) 433–1740 between the hours of 8 A.M. and 5 P.M. Pacific Time, and ask for Jossey-Bass CD-ROM Technical Support.

Please have the following information available:

- Type of computer and operating system
- Version of Windows or Mac OS being used
- Any error messages displayed
- Complete description of the problem.

(It is best if you are sitting at your computer when making the call.)

ASSESSMENTS

A Collection of 50 Questionnaires, Instruments, and Inventories

Bonnie Burn • Maggi Payment

Jossey-Bass
Pfeiffer
San Francisco

Library of Congress Cataloging-in-Publication Data

Burn, Bonnie E.

    Assessments A to Z : a collection of 50 questionnaires, instruments, and inventories /
Bonnie Burn, Maggi Payment.

        p. cm.

    ISBN 0-7879-4509-9

    1. Employees—Training of. 2. Training. I. Payment, Maggi. II. Title.

    [HF5549.5.T7 B795 2000]

    658.3'124—dc21   00-026940

Printed in the United States of America

Published by

Jossey-Bass
Pfeiffer
350 Sansome Street, 5th Floor
San Francisco, California 94104–1342
(415) 433–1740; Fax (415) 433–0499
(800) 274–4434; Fax (800) 569–0443

Visit our website at: www.pfeiffer.com

Acquiring Editor: Matthew Holt
Director of Development: Kathleen Dolan Davies
Developmental Editor: Susan Rachmeler
Senior Production Editor: Pamela Berkman
Manufacturing Supervisor: Becky Carreño

Printing 10 9 8 7 6 5 4 3 2 1

 This book is printed on acid-free, recycled stock that meets or exceeds the minimum GPO and EPA requirements for recycled paper.

"We need the training yesterday!"

"Cut your training time from four hours to two hours!"

"Make sure participants like the training!"

Sound familiar? Then this book is dedicated to you, the brave people who wear the "training hat." Our purpose is to provide you with a quick training resource for getting a jump start on the results you need. These topics and tools were designed to serve you as you continue to serve your organizations and to make a positive difference in the workplace.

With much admiration,

Bonnie Burn
Maggi Payment

Contents

PART 3

Preface

Thirty years ago, workplace training programs typically lasted several days at an offsite location. Today the same training topic is often covered in less than half a day at the job site. In the future, many skills will be taught on personal desktop computers in segments of only a few minutes at the time needed.

However, today's trainers continue to require tools that provide fast and effective ways to promote awareness, feedback, and discussion and that provide information about trainee attitudes, behaviors, preferences, strengths, weaknesses, and learning gaps. Brief assessments (questionnaires, instruments, and inventories) are popular solutions for these purposes.

In our training experiences, the authors have found that short, self-scorable assessments are practical and effective tools. Although many such tools are available for trainers, they are often not suitable for our needs. They may be too complex, too lengthy, or too personal and threatening for respondents. They may be incomplete, they may have challenging scoring systems, or they may be awkward to implement.

In situations in which we have been unable to locate an appropriate instrument for our training goals, we have invented one. In this book we share many of our creations with you. Still better, the accompanying CD-ROM enables you to customize our instruments and make them exactly what you and your trainees need.

IS THIS BOOK FOR YOU?

This one-of-a-kind collection of face-value instruments is designed to help you whether you are

- A novice or experienced trainer,
- An external or internal trainer,
- An accidental trainer such as a technical expert or subject-matter expert, or
- An occasional trainer such as a manager or supervisor.

All instruments in this collection are short and to the point. They are arranged alphabetically by topic for ease of use and can be completed and scored in anywhere from five to fifteen minutes. Within each assessment we have included fewer, rather than more, items. This enables trainers to allocate valuable training time to discussing what the results mean, rather than using so much time to take and score the instrument itself.

A wide range of topics is included in this collection. These topics are taught in all types of organizations to improve worker performance. We have included topics for employee development trainers, management trainers, software trainers, and trainers with a variety of other types of assignments.

Trainers will find topics in this collection that can be helpful in large-group sessions as well as in individual coaching sessions. Topics are included that focus on personal development as well as on professional development. There are suitable topics for self-assessment, worker assessment, management assessment, team assessment, and organizational assessment.

The Topic and Assessment Matrix, found on page 23, is intended to help guide your selection of the appropriate assessments for a particular training program.

If you are new to the value and versatility of brief assessments, you will find information about how to use assessments and when to avoid using them, techniques for customizing or designing your own assessments, tips for facilitation of group discussions, and more, in Parts I and III of this book.

HOW THE BOOK IS ORGANIZED

The book is organized into three parts: introductory material and facilitation strategies for using assessments in Part I, fifty assessments in Part II, and ideas for customizing and designing your own instruments in Part III. The accompanying CD-ROM provides each of the fifty instruments and a checklist for the trainer in an easy-to-customize format.

As is common practice for trainers, the authors have used words such as "instrument," "assessment," "inventory," and "questionnaire" somewhat interchangeably throughout this collection.

Part I

Part I provides background and skill building for trainers who will use the assessments in this collection. It contains an overview of why trainers use them, methods and strategies for trainers to improve their training designs, descriptions of situations that are not appropriate for the use of instruments, suggested trainer qualifications for using instruments (including a short self-assessment for the trainer), technical aspects such as validity, a six-step process for ensuring successful experiences in workshops, and the roles and responsibilities of facilitators and some suggested facilitation methods.

Part II

There are fifty brief assessments in Part II, arranged alphabetically by topic. Each includes a short introduction, instructions for completion and scoring, interpretation information, and questions for consideration. These questions can be given to respondents to complete after taking the assessment in question, or they may be used for discussion.

The instruments are in a variety of formats, including true/false, multiple choice, and rating scales. Each includes everything needed to present it, complete it, and score it. It is up to the trainer to be sure that the respondents' comments are dealt with through discussion and debriefing.

Part III

Part III details strategies to help trainers customize or design instruments to match the needs of their trainees and training programs. A checklist is provided for the trainer to ensure high-quality customized instruments. (This checklist is also on the CD-ROM.) Seven steps necessary for designing short, self-scorable instruments on your own are given.

Watch Your Words! includes information to increase your awareness of common pitfalls of customizing and designing your own instruments. There are tips about using the proper tone for instruments, avoiding offensive terminology, and not violating copyrights and trademarks.

The CD-ROM

The convenient CD-ROM that accompanies this book is copyright-free to purchasers. It is also customizable; trainers can locate and completely customize all instruments by adding, changing, or deleting material. Logos, clip art, and other design features also may be added for total customization of instruments.

February 2000

Bonnie Burn
La Jolla, California

Maggi Payment
San Diego, California

Acknowledgments

For the busy and generous people who gave their time, attention, and insights to this project, we are so grateful. Thank you Matt Holt, Jossey-Bass/Pfeiffer senior editor, for believing in this project and relaying the "just right" words of encouragement to ensure that our book made it to the finish line. You're a winner!

Our editors and production specialists also deserve our thanks for adding their talents to our team. And we wish to thank all our trainees who helped us (or forced us) to create assessments for them over the years.

Bonnie especially wishes to thank Mary Schiffman, Ph.D. Throughout the development of this book you provided that one all-important perspective—"reality checks." God bless you!

Maggi owes special thanks to Alan Payment for his encouragement and assistance. Also, thanks to Cathy Bolger, John Curran, Mary Heikkenin, and Ann and Mary-Ellen Kirkbride for their invaluable assistance.

ASSESSMENTS

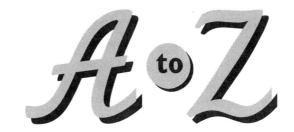

Part 1

INTRODUCTION

How do effective trainers encourage involvement and active participation from trainees? How do trainers know when participants have learned the program content? Savvy trainers use special tools called by various names, including assessments, questionnaires, instruments, and inventories. They use these to help people focus on information about themselves and their work situations and then to use the information for performance improvement.

Brief assessments, questionnaires, instruments, and inventories usually pose minimal personal threat to trainees. People who complete a self-scorable instrument accept and trust the information that comes from it. Because they provided the responses, they are unlikely to discount the results—or even the next steps in a well-designed training program.

When using brief instruments, trainers ask respondents to focus on an attitude, skill, or behavior to estimate what the respondents already believe or know about a topic. This forms the foundation for trainees to acquire new learning and apply it to improving their performance at work. This process can also become the basis for performance improvement across an entire organization.

Short instruments such as those provided in this collection are not intended to predict or prove anything. They are primarily designed and used for the following purposes:

- To focus trainees on a single topic
- To promote engagement with a topic
- To stimulate group discussion of a topic
- To prompt individual insights and learning
- To encourage positive workplace behavior changes

There are many ways for trainers to use and maximize training results with short, to-the-point instruments.

WHY WE USE ASSESSMENTS

Adults learn best when they are actively engaged in the learning process. With the fast pace of the workplace today and the quick development of new products, services, and procedures, workers are continually called on to improve their performance. Assessments are the perfect tools for engaging learners quickly and for beginning the performance improvement process.

Brief instruments provide several benefits for trainers. Among the most important benefits are the following:

- A self-evaluation of a trainee's skills, abilities, or attitudes
- A quick picture of what people already know about a topic
- A quick picture of what people do not know about a topic
- A quick reading of trainees' attitudes about a topic
- Immediate focus and a shared vocabulary about a topic
- Added variety in training program design
- A positive group experience with open discussions
- Lowered resistance to considering change

WAYS TO USE ASSESSMENTS

Trainers use assessments in a variety of ways to help meet performance improvement goals. Typically assessments are completed and scored by participants who then review and discuss their results in a group setting with a trainer or facilitator. However, trainers often use assessments for individual performance coaching as well.

Assessments can also be used before, during, and after training programs in any of the following ways.

Before a Training Session Begins
- To discover participants' perceptions of their skills
- To determine what participants know about a topic
- To determine what participants need to know to be more effective
- To increase awareness about a topic
- To determine level of proficiency with certain skills
- To measure current skills and attitudes
- To estimate parameters of learning needs within a group
- To create or maintain interest in a training session

At the Beginning of a Training Session
- To warm up participants to the training topic
- To increase comfort level of participants
- To focus attention on the training topic
- To generate enthusiasm about a topic
- To engage participants in a training session
- To start a discussion about a specific topic
- To clarify the importance of a topic

- To build cohesiveness and rapport within a group
- To establish a common vocabulary
- To teach skills and information

At Any Time During a Training Session

- To add variety to the training design
- To change the pace from lecture or discussion format
- To energize participants
- To transition between topics
- To measure performance or progress
- To integrate insights into everyday behavior
- To reinforce a topic
- To introduce new training material
- To teach new skills and information
- To practice using skills and information

After a Training Session

- To assess performance change
- To reinforce learning

WHEN TO AVOID USING ASSESSMENTS

Assessments provide many positive benefits, but there are circumstances under which it is best to avoid using them. For example, it is best to avoid using assessments in the following situations:

- When participants are openly negative about the topic. Data gathering and discussion will be contaminated in negative environments. Establish a trusting environment for participants before using an instrument.
- When there will be no opportunity for feedback to respondents who provided the information.
- When trainees are likely to perceive that they are being manipulated for purposes of the organization or the trainer.
- When there is no plan for following up and discussing the information that respondents provide.
- If they are being used to fill time or entertain. For participants to take instruments seriously, set the proper tone.
- If they are being used to put identifying labels on participants. Discourage the use of inappropriate labeling of participants and behaviors.

- If they are being used to gather data for management purposes without telling participants what you are doing.

- If they are being used as a stand-alone training design. The instruments in this book are intended only as components of training designs.

One additional situation can be challenging, but it can be expected, and handled with ease. Occasionally participants with highly analytical mind-sets are likely to focus on the details of an instrument, its items, and the scoring mechanism. Remind these respondents that the instrument is a simple data-gathering tool designed to trigger insight and ideas on the topic. Encourage them to complete and score the instrument with the others in the group.

QUALIFICATIONS FOR USING THIS COLLECTION

There are no special academic or certification courses required before a trainer can use the instruments in this collection. They can be administered by anyone who is willing to establish an accepting and encouraging environment for participants in a training session. However, trainers do need to be comfortable soliciting and discussing the personal experiences, opinions, and ideas of participants in a group setting.

Participants expect that the instruments in a training program will prove to be relevant and useful for their workplace concerns. Trainers who are prepared for delivering the training topic will have sufficient content knowledge to be successful using these instruments.

Because much participant learning depends on the training skills and personal style of their trainers, the following brief self-assessment will help you prepare to use the instruments in this collection most effectively.

Instructions. Circle T (True) or F (False) for each of the following items.

T F 1. Trainers are expected to select the most appropriate instrument for each specific training situation.

T F 2. The word "test" can be substituted for self-development questionnaire, instrument, or inventory.

T F 3. Instruments that are not scientifically validated can only be used to fill time or for amusement during training programs.

T F 4. Because short instruments are not psychological assessments, there is no need to discuss confidentiality of participant results and opinions.

T F 5. There is no reason to "sell" the selected instrument to training participants.

T F 6. Trainers who complete and score an instrument themselves are better prepared to respond to trainee questions about the instrument.

Assessments A to Z/© 2000 Jossey-Bass/Pfeiffer

T F   7. Sharing your personal scores from an instrument with trainees and soliciting feedback about those scores is not appropriate.

T F   8. To obtain the most value from a selected instrument, administer it at the beginning of a training session.

T F   9. Trainers can expect that some people will be indifferent or even opposed to completing a selected instrument.

T F 10. Plan to spend about three minutes going over results and scores from brief assessments.

T F 11. After participants score an instrument, trainers will obtain a convenient label to use for each participant during the remainder of the training program.

T F 12. When participants have concerns about the mismatch between their self-image and data from the instrument, assure them that the instrument is right.

Scoring and Interpretation

The correct responses are explained below.

1. True. Always consider the needs and goals of a specific group and match these to an appropriate instrument. Ensure that your selected instrument does what is needed for a particular group.

2. False. Avoid using the word "test" at all times. It may trigger unpleasant grade-school memories that interfere with participation and learning.

3. False. Instruments do not have to be rigorously tested in controlled circumstances to be useful for training programs. Face validity is all that is required.

4. False. It is a good idea to secure participant agreement that confidentiality is expected from everyone. People generally have differing levels of comfort with self-disclosure: What one person would tell all coworkers, another person wouldn't tell a best friend. Agreement about level of expected confidentiality creates a safer and more open learning environment. Also, trainers must avoid reporting confidential information to managers.

5. False. "Selling" your selected instrument to participants influences their willingness to complete the instrument and gain personal value from it. Selling means explaining the features of the instrument and the benefits your participants will receive from it.

6. True. Trainers are urged to complete and score selected instruments prior to administering them to others. This experience provides an understanding of the scoring system, brings possible misinterpretations to light, and helps make clear how the instrument fits into the context of the planned training session.

7. False. It is often appropriate to share your personal scores and discuss them. This is a way to create openness and trust. It also shows that the instrument is nonthreatening.

8. False. There is no ideal time to use an instrument in a training program design. Timing is influenced by program goals and participant needs; however, it is important to integrate the selected instrument into the overall program design.

9. True. Often a trainer must generate enthusiasm, overcome objections, and assure participants about the intended use of an instrument. Variables that affect acceptance of a selected instrument include gender, age, role within the organization, and personal history. Assure participants that the selected instrument is intended as a self-development experience that does not require them to reveal anything they do not wish to reveal.

10. False. Discussion of opinions, experiences, and scores takes longer than administering and scoring the instrument, perhaps twice as long. Although there are no absolute minimum or maximum times recommended for discussion, it is important to allow sufficient time for all respondents to consider the meaning of their scores. This is where the learning takes place.

11. False. Even when a trainer could label people according to their results, it is never a good idea to do so. In fact, it is a good idea to remind respondents that the information they have is not intended to label them. Discourage trainees from labeling one another.

12. False. Watch for participants who are experiencing mismatches. Assure them that their scores only reflect the answers they selected for a set of questions at a particular time. When there is a lingering concern, suggest that participants discuss it with someone they respect, because sometimes it is difficult to be objective about ourselves.

If you answered ten to twelve items correctly, you are prepared to use the assessments in this collection with much success. If you answered seven to nine items correctly, you will increase your skills and confidence for using assessments as you finish reading Part I of this book. If you answered fewer than seven items correctly, you may wish to read some other material about using instruments in addition to the rest of Part I, such as the Introduction to Inventories, Questionnaires, and Surveys section of the 1999 edition of the *Reference Guide to Handbooks and Annuals* (Jossey-Bass/Pfeiffer, 1999).

WHAT ABOUT VALIDITY?

Terms such as "factor analysis" and "standard deviation" are intentionally missing from this collection. The instruments in this book are not designed to predict behavior of people at work, nor are they concerned with applying psychological theory and research. Instead, they measure what they say they are measuring—attitudes and behaviors of people at work, at a single point in time.

All of the assessments in this book are simple self-assessments with face validity only. They are designed for use by training participants who will first complete the items, then review and discuss their results with others. The purpose is to increase respondents' self-awareness and to generate ideas for learning and performance improvement.

The instruments are considered valid when the data serve the trainer's purposes—and when respondents believe their results are useful, reasonably accurate descriptions of their attitudes, beliefs, or behavior.

Selecting Instruments with Face Validity

To select an instrument with face validity only, it is important for trainers to consider the following six questions:

1. Does this instrument measure attitudes and/or behaviors of people at work?
2. Will this instrument serve the objectives of my training program?
3. Will this instrument increase self-awareness and lead to performance improvement?
4. Can this instrument increase respondents' effectiveness at work?
5. Is this instrument appropriate for this person or this group?
6. Is it easy for participants to complete and score the items?

Four Technical Considerations

To monitor the appropriateness of instruments you select or modify, evaluate the items for the following:

- *Applicability.* Can trainees relate to the items? Do items reflect real-life experiences of trainees? Do words or phrases require modification?
- *Complexity.* Are the ideas too complicated? Is the instrument too long or too short? Is the scoring simple? Is the time allowed for completion realistic?
- *Language Level.* Is the language clear? Is the language appropriately technical or non-technical? Is the reading level appropriate?
- *Offensiveness.* Are the items offensive because of language, concept, tone, or for any other reason? Will the instrument be nonthreatening to all participants?

SIX STEPS TO SUCCESS

Although the assessments in this collection can be used for individual coaching or counseling situations, they are intended for use in group settings. The following six steps provide a guide for busy trainers as they prepare to use instruments with groups of any size.

Step 1. Preparing

- Consider selecting an assessment, inventory, or questionnaire only if using one supports the established objectives for the training program.

- Determine when during the training program you will use a selected instrument.

- Identify and review possible instruments for relevance to your needs.

- Complete, score, and evaluate your personal experience with the instruments you select.

- Consider appropriateness of the selected instruments for the overall training design.

- Consider asking key individuals to complete and score the instrument to provide feedback and recommendations.

- Plan modifications of an instrument, if needed.

- Prepare instruments for use, along with any other materials such as overheads, pencils, and props.

- Anticipate trainee reactions and develop ideas for responding to them.

Step 2. Positioning and Introducing

- Put participants in a positive, cooperative mood.

- Explain how the instrument will benefit participants.

- Explain why you are using the instrument.

- Describe how the instrument fits into the entire training session.

- Avoid saying the word *test*.

- Provide clear and simple instructions, then check for understanding.

- Ask trainees to suspend judgment, to complete and score the assessment, and to expect to discuss the results when everyone has finished.

Step 3. Completing

- Tell participants you will walk around the room to answer individual questions as they are completing the instrument.

- Make sure participants are following instructions correctly.

- Remind participants that there is no need to rush through the instrument.

- As participants complete the instrument, observe their behaviors.

- Make notes of your observations and other items to discuss when everyone has completed the instrument.

- Discourage interruptions while participants complete the instrument.

- Limit your involvement with participants while they complete the instrument.

- Ask participants who want to discuss something that will interrupt others to join you in the hallway to talk.

Assessments A to Z/© 2000 Jossey-Bass/Pfeiffer

Step 4. Scoring

- Mingle with participants to ensure that everyone is correctly scoring the instrument.
- Remind participants that there is sufficient time for this activity and not to be pressured by those who finish early.
- Ask participants who finish early to wait for everyone to finish. (Expect most participants to complete brief assessments at nearly the same time. You may want to have additional reading material available for early finishers.)

Step 5. Interpreting and Discussing

- Ask positive questions about participants' experiences with the instrument.
- Facilitate a discussion to assist participants with understanding their own scores compared with their predictions about their scores or the group's average score.
- If appropriate, remind participants that today's scores are like a thermometer reading that could be different tomorrow.
- Share observations you made while participants were completing the instrument.
- Solicit as many of participants' opinions and comments as possible.
- Use participants' comments to link the instrument to the objectives of the training session.
- Ask for real-life examples from their work situations.
- If group discussion strays, remind participants about the reasons for using the instrument during the training session.
- Remind participants that all scores are confidential within the group and that reporting to others outside the group is not acceptable.
- Offer to meet with participants who have a conflict between their scores and their self-image.
- Refer to "Group Facilitation of Assessments" (below) for additional techniques.

Step 6. Summarizing

- Thank participants for their participation and comments.
- Summarize major ways the instrument supports objectives of the training session.
- Reiterate anything significant from this experience that will encourage further learning during the training session.
- Segue to the next activity.

GROUP FACILITATION OF ASSESSMENTS

While people complete and score an assessment, their focus is on the items of that assessment as well as their own thoughts and feelings about the items. At the same time, trainers are moving into a *facilitator* role.

The facilitator's role is not the same as a traditional trainer's role. While an instrument is being completed, a trainer-as-facilitator begins to observe what is and what is not happening within the group. For example, a facilitator will notice who is engaged, who appears to be distracted, and who appears concerned about something.

After the group has completed and scored an instrument, facilitators coax and guide a discussion of respondents' ideas, opinions, and concerns related to the results. These facilitated discussions enable respondents to consider the meaning of their data and to compare ideas with one another. During these discussions facilitators often find opportunities to present material they planned to teach, so they move back and forth between the roles of facilitator and trainer, discussion leader and teacher.

Facilitators interact with trainees in a trusting personal way, so they must have excellent interpersonal skills. The following words are often used to describe effective facilitators:

- Goal-oriented
- Respectful
- Flexible
- Proactive
- Responsive
- Resilient
- Open to feedback
- Multi-tasker
- Role model
- Positive reinforcer
- Catalyst

Responsibilities of Facilitators

The responsibilities of facilitators include the following:

- To provoke thought about and discussion on the topic
- To encourage all group members to participate
- To broaden the perspectives of individuals
- To probe for personal meaning to individuals
- To offer observations of what is and is not happening within the group
- To listen actively and be comfortable with silences
- To establish eye contact with individuals to draw them into the group
- To analyze and synthesize information and ask clarifying questions
- To suggest appropriate behaviors based on ideas and insights expressed
- To keep the group discussion on topic

How to Facilitate

Using their observations and skills, and some hunches, facilitators prompt participant discussion and learning. Facilitators observe what happens as participants interact in order to discover useful information such as:

- Who is participating and who is not
- Areas of apparent conflict and concern for participants
- Who appears to have influence over others
- Who is cooperative and who is antagonistic

Facilitators then ask questions to provoke dialogue. Specific questions get the best results. Typically, facilitators find it helpful to plan several questions in advance before meeting with a group.

Facilitators continually probe for specific examples and illustrations. They repeatedly ask, "What experiences have you had that illustrate that for us?" and "What examples of that can you share with us?" They are careful to use only open-ended questions that cannot be answered with a simple yes or no.

Additionally, effective facilitators state and model the level of participation they expect, the amount of openness they want, and their expectations around confidentiality. For example, a facilitator may say, "We all learn the most when each person contributes to the discussion. Of course, I don't expect you to reveal anything you are not comfortable saying here. I also expect that what we discuss in this room will not be repeated to people elsewhere. Does anyone have any comments about these expectations?"

Facilitators are not members of the group, and their role is to promote focused discussion by group members. Their personal opinions and preferences about topics and specific participant comments are usually irrelevant to the group discussion. However, facilitators may use part of a group discussion as a jumping-off point for teaching a segment of the training material. The best facilitators are always on the lookout for these training opportunities during facilitated discussions.

Facilitators help participants share their views openly and constructively. They do not prevent participants from expressing negative feelings, but they also do not permit verbal attacks and lengthy negative monologues.

Because facilitators are not mediators or judges, they must avoid resolving disputes within the group. It is appropriate to point out that the group is not an appropriate forum for certain discussions and to suggest an alternative way to handle the disagreement. Facilitators often model a new way of disagreeing for participants by saying, "Let's agree to disagree on this point and move on to the next point."

Tasks for Facilitators: Before, During, After

Before participants complete an instrument, effective facilitators take three important steps.

1. *Position the instrument for acceptance.* Most adults in training prefer to know

- Why they are being asked to do something
- What they can expect to receive from doing what is asked of them
- How what is requested of them fits into the big picture of their job

Effective facilitators discuss each of these items thoroughly with participants. They also invite participant questions and concerns before an instrument is administered.

2. *Involve everyone in the group.* Be aware that all participants do not come to training willingly. Those who are hostile, too busy with other work, or who think they already know everything they need to know about the topic must be converted to group members who are ready to participate. Otherwise, you can expect negative remarks, interruptions, angry challenges, and other unpleasant disturbances.

3. *Give clear and simple instructions and verify understanding.* After giving instructions, ask: "What questions do you have before we begin?" Clear up all misunderstandings and concerns before anyone begins the instrument.

During the time participants are completing and scoring an instrument, effective facilitators do the following:

1. *Observe participants and make notes.* These are for discussion after everyone completes the instrument. Facilitators watch for the following behaviors:

- Are participants engaged?
- Do participants fidget?
- Do participants look around at others?
- Are participants talking to one another?

These observed behaviors form the basis for discussion questions about the relevance of the instrument for participants. For example, facilitators may ask participants whether they feel that completing the instrument was helpful, whether they liked it, or whether anyone liked taking it.

2. *Mingle to observe behaviors of participants more closely.* Trust and confidence in facilitators usually is increased by such physical proximity. Tell them you will walk around to do "professional eavesdropping." However, discourage participants from having conversations with you or anyone else at this time.

3. *Avoid interrupting participants.* While moving around the room, professional facilitators avoid making comments, moving furniture, or doing anything else that might divert participants' attention away from the instrument.

4. *Coach a participant only when necessary.* Facilitators avoid disturbing other participants when one person has a question. They either ask for a private discussion away from the entire group or suggest saving the matter for group discussion when everyone has finished.

After participants have scored their instruments, facilitators use their special skills in the following ways:

- To begin the group discussion
- To keep the discussion going at a good pace
- To keep the discussion focused on objectives
- To keep the discussion constructive
- To encourage everyone to participate
- To discourage people from monopolizing the conversation
- To build respondents' confidence
- To summarize for the group
- To segue to the next part of the training program

Questions Facilitators Ask

As mentioned earlier, effective facilitation is the key to success when using brief assessments. Asking the right questions is a very important aspect of facilitation. Effective facilitators have a flexible repertoire of questions to help participants analyze, discuss, and learn from an assessment. Good questions also keep a discussion going and keep it on track.

Facilitators ask themselves certain questions while they are observing participants. They reserve other questions to ask participants. Experiment with the following questions as you begin to build your own repertoire of effective questions.

Sample Questions Facilitators Ask Themselves

- Is the room creating distractions and detractions for this group?
- Is the atmosphere in the room enthusiastic, hostile, unconcerned, or something else?
- Does the group size encourage or discourage open discussion?
- Is anything needed to get people involved?
- Who is and who is not participating?
- Are people preoccupied?
- Who draws others into the discussion?
- Who interrupts others?
- Who keeps others from talking?
- What body language is exhibited by people?
- Do participants share personal information?

- How are the quiet people being treated?
- Who is ignored when speaking?
- Who influences others?
- Are there leadership struggles?
- Is there enough time left?

Sample Questions Facilitators Ask Participants
- Can you elaborate on that?
- What would you prefer?
- Good point. And another example would be . . . ?
- That is one way. Another way could be . . . ?
- Can you tell us a few specifics?
- Can you explain that for us in a different way?
- Would you describe a particular situation in which this is true (omitting names, of course)?
- Would this be helpful?
- In what ways would this be helpful?
- Are you saying this plan needs more work?
- Who would use this strategy?
- How would you use this information?
- What actions can you take to make that happen?

Additionally, facilitators may ask topic-specific questions, such as those provided at the end of each assessment in Part II.

Difficult People and Difficult Situations

Facilitators may encounter difficult participants and difficult situations when using instruments. Ignoring difficult participants and situations does not make them go away. Difficulties happen for a reason. Ask participants for explanations of their behavior, even when you think you know the answers. Avoid sarcasm and patronizing remarks, and assertively ask for behavior that serves the interests of the entire group. The following options are useful for some of the most common types of challenging participants and situations.

Complainers
- Actively listen to complaints and then summarize them for the group.
- Ask the group whether they share the same complaint.
- If there is something wrong that you can fix, fix it.

- If it is a private matter, ask to discuss it privately at the next break.
- If there is no other option, "agree to disagree" with the complainer by asking, "Could we agree to disagree about this and move on to the next point?" Then quickly move on.

Monopolizers

- Tactfully interrupt with a question or summarizing statement and move on;
- Ask for a volunteer who has not said anything so far;
- Ask for a volunteer who has not said anything in a while;
- Ask "Who else has an idea?" and call on another speaker;
- Announce that each speaker must now add something new to a previous idea;
- Change to a pairs or trios activity; or
- Arrange to speak privately with a monopolizer to ask for the behavior you want.

Nontalkers

- Arrange a pairs activity and ask people who have not been speaking to be the reporters.
- Arrange a pairs activity and semi-privately ask people who have not been speaking, "Would you mind sharing the information from your pair with the entire group?"
- Ask a question and direct participants to discuss their responses with two others near them before the entire group discusses the responses.
- Ask to hear from someone who has not yet spoken while you are making sweeping eye contact around the room.
- Ask, "Has everyone had a chance to say something to us about this topic?"

When Someone Offers a "Wrong" Answer

- Acknowledge the participant's comment.
- Ask the group if someone else has another idea.
- Explore possible responses with the group.
- Correct the information or behavior before moving to the next point in a way that maintains the self-esteem of the participant with the "wrong" answer.

When Sideline Discussions Are Disruptive

- Arrange a pairs activity and semi-privately ask sideline talkers whether the matter they are discussing would be of interest to the rest of the group. If not, ask them to join the rest of the group and leave private discussions for breaks.
- Walk over and stand by the sideline talkers. Usually they will stop talking as you approach them.

When You Want Participants to Move

- Ask participants to move to different seats or tables at natural break times, such as after refreshment or meal breaks or after an activity when they have been away from their seats.

- Remind participants that change is the norm at work and that it helps to be flexible and open to change. Point out that moving to a different seat may be one of the easiest changes they will be asked to make this week.

- Remind participants that moving around gives them a chance to meet different people and hear new ideas.

Twenty-Five Tips for Facilitating Instrumentation

1. Participants who are comfortable with one another are more likely to discuss their results and ideas openly, so it is generally most effective to use introductions and icebreakers before using instruments.

2. Arrange seating to minimize the number of people with their backs to one another.

3. Use participants' names as much as possible. Name tents and stick-on name badges provide names everyone can see.

4. Positive wording of questions is more effective than negative wording. Say, "How many agree with your results?" instead of "How many disagree with your results?"

5. Listen closely and acknowledge all ideas of participants; thank people for sharing their ideas; and avoid judging anyone's ideas.

6. While participants are talking, list their responses for everyone to see. You may use a flip chart, an overhead projector, or the latest technology for this.

7. Express your confidence in the abilities of the group and group members. Say something such as, "That's a good way to do that. Does anyone have another way?"

8. Seek opportunities to draw each person into the group discussion at some point. When the group is too large for everyone to have a chance to speak, ask for trios to discuss something for three minutes.

9. Tell personal anecdotes, but avoid telling too many of them. Vary your stories so group members with diverse interests and backgrounds can relate to them, for example, avoid stories that are all about cooking or all about baseball.

10. Ask participants to share their experiences, but ask different people each time. During a pairs activity draw quiet people into the discussion by asking, "Would you mind giving the group your thoughts on this?"

11. Ask group members to respond to participant questions, even when you could answer them yourself. Ask something like, "Does anyone have a thought on this?" It is only appropriate to offer your own response when you are sure no one else has a response.

12. Ask probing questions to bring out information and ideas, for example: "How does that work?" "Do you have any advice for doing this?" or "Has anyone else had experience with this sort of thing?"

13. Refer back to what someone said earlier, for example, "That's similar to what Lee told us about earlier."

14. Focus on the *behaviors* of participants instead of on what you perceive to be their personalities or attitudes. Say, "I noticed Lee walked away from your table, and I wondered how that changed the conversation." Don't say something like, "Lee is a jerk."

15. Point out positive behaviors and their effect on improving performance. Remember that what is rewarded gets repeated. Praise lavishly.

16. When offering praise, explain why. In this way, everyone can learn from the situation.

17. Admit to being human, too. Explain that everyone makes mistakes when learning something new.

18. Be a role model for being a willing student. Learn from your participants, and thank them for sharing their information, ideas, and insights.

19. Acknowledge correct answers with enthusiasm. When participants offer wrong answers, acknowledge their responses and tactfully offer correct answers so that participants learn, for example, "Many people thought that too; however, what works better is. . . ."

20. Use neutral body language. Avoid crossing your arms over your chest and other postures that could be interpreted as approval or disapproval. Watch any tendencies you have to shift your weight or move to another spot in the room when something pleases or displeases you.

21. Avoid facial expressions that could indicate disapproval or approval of people, their ideas, and their opinions. Facilitators who give away their negative feelings and thoughts because they have an expressive face or personality can benefit from coaching. Acting lessons are also helpful.

22. Walk around the room and stand near people. Closing the physical distance between yourself and the participants narrows the psychological distance as well. Participants feel drawn into the group, and they become more willing to participate.

23. Be sensitive to participants who prefer not to talk publicly about their thoughts and feelings on a topic. Honor their choice for privacy and avoid focusing any attention on that choice.

24. Maintain control of the group and the training agenda at all times. It may become necessary to remind the group of the time, the need to stay on the topic, and so forth. Say something like, "I think you should know we only have ten minutes remaining before our lunch break."

25. Briefly summarize the discussion of the instrument and then segue to the next topic or activity. A segue is a transition that enables participants to go smoothly from one part of the training to another part. An example is, "I think you will find that the next part of our training builds on this discussion. Let's go into the next room to watch a short video."

Part 2

TOPIC AND ASSESSMENT MATRIX

Trainers and facilitators like to select assessments that will engage participants in the topic. The assessments presented in this book are not intended as a substitute for a training program, but each can be included as a piece of a well-designed learning program. Trainers can provide additional information and learning experiences on each topic, incorporating the assessment carefully.

The following matrix matches training topics with the specific assessments in this collection. In the column on the left are general topics that are often presented in training programs. Listed in the next columns are subtopics, the specific assessments found in this collection, and the page numbers on which they appear. Each assessment may be listed a number of times, according to different topics or subtopics one might be interested in.

Main Topic	Subtopic	Title	Page
Business Writing	Business Writing	Is Your Business Writing Streamlined?	41
	E-mail	What Do You Need to Learn About Writing and Managing E-Mail?	59
	Letters & Memo Writing	Is It Time to Check Your Letter Writing Skills?	111
	Buzz Words (zzBuzz Words)	Do You Understand Buzz Words?	219
Career Planning	Job Satisfaction	Are You Satisfied with Your Job?	95
	Job Search	Do You Have Up-to-Date Job Search Skills?	99
	Mentoring	What Do Mentors Do?	121
	Negotiation	Do You Know How to Negotiate for a Pay Increase?	125
	Networking	How Could You Use Networking for Job Advancement?	127

Assertiveness

Are You Assertive?

Assertiveness helps people express their needs in a way that is acceptable to others. Most of the time people are cooperative and thoughtful. However, when conflict arises, people respond in different ways. Some act aggressively, some passively, and some assertively. See what you know about assertion by taking the following assessment.

Instructions   Circle the letter for the response that, in your opinion, best answers each of the following questions.

1. You are in a long line to pay for your lunch. Someone walks up and moves into line in front of you. The assertive thing to do is

    a. to complain to others around you in a loud voice

    b. to ask the person to go to the end of the line

2. Which of the following is not a reason to be assertive?

    a. to achieve your goals

    b. to show who is right

3. Assertive people show empathy. Empathy is

    a. understanding that another person's experience is valid from his or her own point of view

    b. waiting until the other person stops speaking before offering your advice

4. The definition of assertiveness usually includes the following

    a. "deny the rights of others"

    b. "ask for what you want"

5. Which type of statement below is considered an assertiveness technique?

   a. "You" statements

   b. "I" statements

6. A nonassertive person may respond to a situation with nonverbal cues such as

   a. a whiny voice

   b. direct eye contact

7. Aggressive words from others violate your right to courtesy and respect. Which of the following is an aggressive comment?

   a. "Don't be such a fool."

   b. "Would you mind very much if we skip the formalities?"

8. Which of the following is *not* an assertive way to begin a statement?

   a. "I, uh, wonder . . ."

   b. "I want . . ."

9. Assertive communication allows you to speak up for your rights without violating the rights of others in which of the following situations?

   a. only at home

   b. situations at work and at home

10. Which of the following is an appropriate assertive response?

    a. keeping your opinions to yourself when you are angry with your boss

    b. saying that your way of doing a task appears to be as good as the other person's

SCORING AND INTERPRETATION

Instructions   The following are the correct responses and the rationale for each of the questions above. Circle any wrong answers you had and write the total number of wrong answers on the line below.

Total: _____

1	b	Assertiveness is asking directly for what you want another person to do.
2	b	Assertive behavior is not about who is right and who is wrong.
3	a	Giving advice is not assertive behavior.
4	b	Assertive behavior never denies the rights of others.
5	b	Beginning a statement with "I" is a useful assertiveness technique.
6	a	Direct eye contact is considered assertive behavior.
7	a	A is clearly a disrespectful statement.
8	a	Assertive statements are direct.
9	b	Assertive communication takes place at home as well as at work.
10	b	Assertiveness involves telling the truth as you see it without being disrespectful.

If you missed zero to one item, you are probably comfortable with what you say to others and take care to be direct and respectful in your communication.

If you missed two to four items, you may believe assertiveness is inappropriate. The assertive response may seem too direct to you, perhaps even hostile, or you may think you must speak your mind bluntly in every case, no matter what the other person feels. You may have communication problems with others who ask you to tell them how you really feel.

If you missed five or more items, you will learn a lot about assertiveness from taking a program on the topic. You can expect to discover that people respond positively to an assertive request or assertive statement. You will also learn the differences among assertive, passive, and aggressive statements, responses, and requests.

QUESTIONS TO CONSIDER

1. In what ways do life experiences have an influence on a person's assertiveness?

2. What do we learn from other people about being assertive, passive, or aggressive?

3. What types of jobs are good matches for assertive people?

4. "Assertiveness can help you maintain a good relationship with your supervisor." Do you agree or disagree with that statement? Why?

5. "You have the right to be treated with respect and to maintain your dignity in every situation." What are your comments about this statement?

Attitude
How Is Your Attitude at Work?

Your attitude makes a difference to your coworkers and customers. Do people enjoy being around you? Do they think you're easy to get along with, or do they think that you're moody or difficult to be around? Check out your attitude by taking the following assessment.

Instructions   Think about your typical behavior at work and write a T for "true" or F for "false" before each of the following statements.

_____ 1. When I have a bad day I am careful not to show my irritation to others.

_____ 2. No matter how busy I am, I am nice to customers and coworkers.

_____ 3. I am willing to delay my break when someone needs my help.

_____ 4. I am pleasant to others even when they are not pleasant to me.

_____ 5. I am courteous and respectful to all customers.

_____ 6. I avoid rude responses, no matter what the other person says to me.

_____ 7. I am not willing to argue with others at work.

_____ 8. I often do things that are not my job.

_____ 9. I like doing my job in a professional manner.

_____ 10. I am positive and friendly with everyone at work.

_____ 11. Even on bad days I am positive and friendly.

_____ 12. I don't let the bad moods of others affect me.

_____ 13. I am proud of being able to get along with others easily.

_____ 14. I am a calm, courteous, and easygoing person.

_____ 15. I believe we all deserve respect from others.

_____ 16. I stay away from people who are negative so I won't participate in the negativity.

_____ 17. I can only do things when I'm in the right mood.

_____ 18. I can't change what I think.

_____ 19. I can't change how I feel.

_____ 20. Other people are responsible for my bad moods.

SCORING AND INTERPRETATION

Congratulations if you answered "true" for items 1 through 16 and "false" for items 17 through 20. People around you probably think you have a wonderful attitude. They are likely to enjoy working with you and to wish everyone had your good attitude. Customers enjoy working with you too.

If you answered "false" for any items from 1 to 16, look carefully at them. Would you enjoy working with someone who responded in that way? If you answered "true" for any items from 17 through 20, your coworkers and customers may wish they could change your attitude and make it easier to work with you. You will learn new things in a training class to help you improve your attitude.

QUESTIONS TO CONSIDER

1. Many people believe our attitudes are fixed at birth. What do you think?

2. Do you think a bad attitude is contagious? Can you describe a time you "caught" a bad attitude from someone?

3. Do you think a good attitude is contagious? Can you describe a time you "caught" a good attitude from someone?

4. When people interact with you during the day at work, what is the attitude they expect from you?

5. Think about the people you most enjoy being with. What words describe their attitudes?

Burnout
Are You a Candidate for Job Burnout?

People think they won't suffer from burnout if they enjoy their work. It's not true. People who are very happy with their work can suffer from job burnout too. Burnout is mental, physical, and emotional exhaustion that builds up over time. Usually a burnout victim is not even aware of having burnout. Check the likelihood of your burning out on the job by taking the following assessment.

Instructions   On the line preceding each of the following statements, rate yourself according to the following scale:

1 = Almost never   2 = Infrequently   3 = About half the time   4 = Usually   5 = Always

_____ 1. I am tired or exhausted when I get up on work days.

_____ 2. I have trouble getting to sleep, waking up, or both.

_____ 3. I am increasingly frustrated, impatient, and irritable at work.

_____ 4. I have work on my mind even when I am not at work.

_____ 5. I am underappreciated at work.

_____ 6. I have difficulty making small decisions at work.

_____ 7. I procrastinate more than in the past.

_____ 8. I make small mistakes in everyday tasks.

_____ 9. My loved ones tell me I am "too intense."

_____ 10. I am in a bad mood more than I am in a good mood.

_____ 11. I am too busy to sit down and enjoy a meal with friends.

_____ 12. I am too busy for leisure activities.

1 = Almost never   2 = Infrequently   3 = About half the time   4 = Usually   5 = Always

____ 13. It is difficult to make "small talk" with people I formerly enjoyed being with.

____ 14. I often lose my personal possessions, such as keys and glasses.

____ 15. I seem to have lost my perspective.

____ 16. I am overwhelmed by all the responsibilities I have.

____ 17. I have insomnia, headaches, hypertension, rashes, or digestive problems.

____ 18. I need help such as alcohol, pills, chocolate, or ice cream to help me cope with stress.

____ 19. I wonder if there is any point to living like this.

____ 20. I have fantasies about getting away from it all.

Total: _____

SCORING AND INTERPRETATION

Instructions   Total your responses to the statements above and put your total on the line provided.

Congratulations if your total is 39 or less. You are successfully avoiding burnout and can probably offer helpful suggestions to others. You are a good manager of your stress level.

If your score is 40 to 59, you are managing your job stress well only some of the time. At other times you are compromising your health and well-being. You must learn ways to repel stressful work situations that can lead to burnout. Continue doing the right things, and do them more often.

If your score is 60 to 79, you are in the burnout danger zone. You suffer from burnout, and your loved ones know it. They may feel miserable around you and frustrated because they cannot help you. Immediately find ways to make changes in your life or you are likely to have serious problems with your well-being and your relationships.

If your score is over 80, you are already in trouble, and you know it. Learning ways to combat burnout is the easy part. Actually practicing ways to combat burnout is the hard part. You must regain control of your work situation now. Do not delay. Your life depends on your rearranging your priorities and responsibilities.

QUESTIONS TO CONSIDER

1. It has been said that burnout is not a state of being, but that it is a symptom—suggesting that your job expectations clash with your everyday work world. What do you think about this idea? What examples of differing expectations have you or your friends experienced?

2. Exhaustion distorts a person's judgment and mood. What is one step you can take to get more rest tonight?

3. The first step to begin to fix a problem is to acknowledge that there is a problem. Why is it so difficult for anyone to acknowledge job burnout?

4. Which worker groups are most likely to suffer job burnout? Why do you think this is true?

5. What are two ways you can offer help and support to someone you care about who suffers from job burnout?

𝓑Business Writing

Is Your Business Writing Streamlined?

Today's busy readers appreciate streamlined writing. Your letters, memos, and e-mail messages must be easy to read and understand. It's your job as the writer to be as clear and concise as possible. Find out whether your writing is streamlined by taking the following quick assessment.

Instructions Match the streamlined word or phrase from Column B with its outdated and redundant phrase in Column A below. Write your answers on the lines beside the numbers in Column A.

Answer	Column A	Column B
_____	1. at this point in time	A. last week
_____	2. came to the conclusion that	B. to
_____	3. consensus of opinion	C. twice
_____	4. due to the fact that	D. now
_____	5. during the course of last week	E. innovations
_____	6. enclosed please find	F. concluded
_____	7. filled to capacity	G. because
_____	8. for the purpose of	H. enclosed is
_____	9. I would like to thank you for	I. for
_____	10. in order to	J. after
_____	11. merged together	K. postponed
_____	12. new innovations	L. consensus

Answer	Column A	Column B
_____	13. on two different occasions	M. merged
_____	14. postponed until later	N. filled
_____	15. subsequent to	O. thank you for

SCORING AND INTERPRETATION

Instructions   The proper answers are given below. Circle each response you marked *incorrectly.*

D   1
F   2
L   3
G   4
A   5
H   6
N   7
I   8
O   9
B   10
M   11
E   12
C   13
K   14
J   15

If you correctly matched all responses, congratulations! Your writing is generally clear and concise and your readers appreciate your efforts.

If you missed one to three answers, your writing will become clearer as you notice your tendency to use wordy and outdated phrases and then change those tendencies.

If you missed four to six answers, your writing needs significant improvement and you would learn a lot from taking a class on business writing.

Questions to Consider

1. What is the origin of outdated and redundant phrases such as the ones above?

2. Computers are quickly changing the ways of business communication. What examples can you give?

3. The rules of grammar change over time. Can you think of any changes in acceptable grammatical usage since you were in high school?

4. Name one important rule you learned from your high school English teacher.

5. In your opinion, is a person who reads books, newspapers, and magazines more likely to have better writing skills than someone who does not? Why or why not?

                                              Assessments A to Z/© 2000 Jossey-Bass/Pfeiffer

Change
How Much Change Have You Experienced at Work?

Change is constant at work today. No one can escape it. Still, too many changes in a short period of time throw most people off balance. See how much change is in your work life by taking the following assessment.

Instructions   Mark an X in front of each workplace change listed below that you have experienced in the past two years.

____   1. I have a new job.

____   2. I have many new job responsibilities.

____   3. I have new coworkers.

____   4. I have a new boss.

____   5. My work environment has changed.

____   6. I received a promotion.

____   7. I did not receive an expected promotion.

____   8. I now supervise my former peers.

____   9. I must use a new or different technology.

____   10. My organization rapidly expanded.

____   11. My organization merged with another organization.

____   12. My organization reduced its workforce.

____   13. My organization has high employee turnover.

____   14. My organization has fewer customers than in the past.

_____ 15. My organization went public.

_____ 16. My organization has new policies and expectations.

_____ 17. My organization seems to be in a different business now.

_____ 18. My team or department reorganized.

_____ 19. My organization reorganized.

_____ 20. My organization is facing fierce competition.

_____ 21. I lost my job because of a layoff.

_____ 22. I changed careers.

Total: _____

SCORING AND INTERPRETATION

Instructions　Total the number of changes you marked and put your total on the rule following the list of statements. If you marked fifteen or more of the changes on this list, you are experiencing an average number of changes for today's work world. Does that surprise you? Today it is routine for people to change jobs, start over in new types of work, and experience a fast-paced, changing work life.

If you marked fewer than ten changes on this list, you are in an unusual workplace because it has not been significantly impacted by technology changes, changing markets, or reorganization.

QUESTIONS TO CONSIDER

1. Look over the statements you marked in this assessment and circle the ones that you did not expect to happen. Were these difficult changes for you, or did you make a smooth transition? How did you react when you first heard about each change? Could there be more unexpected changes in your future work life?

2. Think back to when you started your first job. What were you thinking then about what your future work life would be like?

3. Some people make changes to have things be different and to reduce their boredom. Some people avoid making changes and fight to keep things just as they are. What is your preference? Does your manager have the same preference?

4. Researchers say people can learn to cope with change if they do certain things that increase their resilience. One recommendation is to do things in a different way intentionally. People can go to work via a different route, brush their teeth with a different hand, listen to a different type of music, and so on. What are two different ways of behaving that you are willing to experiment with for a week?

5. Adjusting to changes involves a certain amount of resistance at the start. This resistance may be brief, or it may be prolonged. Think about someone you know (or a character in a book, movie, or play) who experienced a major change. Did this person experience emotional highs and lows? What other emotions did this person experience?

Coaching

What Are Your Views on Coaching Employees?

Coaching employees to succeed takes time, effort, and good skills. It is hard work to be a good coach, and managers have a great deal of other work to do. This assessment will help you to think about your own coaching skills.

Instructions The following statements about coaching opportunities were anonymously provided by a group of managers. Think about your own experiences with your employees over the last six weeks. Circle the number for any of the following items that describes your attitude about coaching on *at least one occasion* during that time period.

1. Employees know what they are supposed to do, and I expect them to do things right.

2. I can't take time for coaching now because I have too many other important things to do.

3. It's too hard to find time to set up a meeting right now.

4. I have too many people reporting to me to spend time with only one person.

5. If one employee doesn't get it right, I'll find another employee who will.

6. This person is a new employee, and it takes a long time to get up to speed.

7. That employee is only an average performer anyway.

8. That employee did not ask for assistance, so I will not offer any.

9. I told that employee once before what to do and once should be enough.

10. I told someone else to help that employee.

11. That employee doesn't seem interested in improving his or her work output.

12. I will feel uncomfortable talking privately with that person about work output.

13. I don't know how to do coaching very well.

14. No one is coaching me on my job.

15. Nobody ever coached me on my job.

SCORING AND INTERPRETATION

Congratulations if you circled only one or two of the item numbers. You are probably a manager who knows the value of coaching employees to improve their performance, and you do coach them. You are also a busy manager and a human being, so you had a time or two when you couldn't do what you thought you should do.

If you circled three or more items, you can benefit from learning more about coaching employees for performance improvement. It is usually worth every minute of your time to coach your employees. You may also be a very busy manager who needs to delegate some of your workload to others.

If you circled more than six items, you are probably painfully honest with yourself and very aware of your shortcomings in the area of coaching employees for performance. You will benefit greatly from the new skills you develop in a coaching class.

QUESTIONS TO CONSIDER

1. What experiences did you have with someone coaching you during your childhood and teen years?

2. Coaching people to perform better at work is a strange idea for some managers. They believe it is a waste of time and that it is better to find a new employee who is a better worker. What do you think about this idea?

3. Coaching usually involves working closely with an employee. What are some things that can happen if the manager and the worker are very different types of people and they do not seem to like one another? What helpful suggestions do you have for them if this is true?

4. Some managers may not know how to give appropriate feedback. What happens when a manager does not give any type of feedback to workers? What is your recommendation for these managers?

5. "Coaching people to do their jobs better takes a lot of time, and it is a waste of time these days when people change jobs so often." What is your response to this statement?

Customer Service
Are You Good with Customers on the Phone?

Providing excellent customer service is both challenging and satisfying, especially when you are on the telephone. How well do you serve customers when you can't see them? Find out by taking the following assessment.

Instructions   Read each statement below and rate your typical telephone behavior according to the following scale:

1 = Always   2 = Usually   3 = Sometimes   4 = Rarely   5 = Never

____ 1. I greet customers with an upbeat greeting.

____ 2. I identify my organization and my department, and I add my name.

____ 3. I ask customers about their requests.

____ 4. If customers are upset, I let them vent before attempting to resolve the issue.

____ 5. If a customer rambles, I tactfully redirect the discussion back to the original request.

____ 6. I take notes while a customer is talking.

____ 7. I ask customers whether I may put them on "hold."

____ 8. I find someone else to help customers if I cannot help them.

____ 9. I clarify my understanding of the customer's needs.

____ 10. I use common words when explaining products and services to customers.

____ 11. I know how to obtain help from the experts for my customers.

____ 12. When saying "no" to a customer, I offer other options.

____ 13. I offer a choice of solutions at every opportunity.

1 = Always   2 = Usually   3 = Sometimes   4 = Rarely   5 = Never

____ 14. I avoid passing off customer problems to my coworkers.

____ 15. I thank customers for asking us to help them.

____ 16. When I say I will follow up, I do so.

____ 17. When I receive important information that will help my callers, I keep it where I can find it.

Total: _____

SCORING AND INTERPRETATION

Instructions   Total your responses and put your total on the line above. The ideal score is 17. Are you close? A score below 20 is excellent. It indicates that your conversations with customers go well for you and for the customers.

If your score is over 35, you will benefit from telephone skills training. You will learn new skills to improve your performance. Your customers will be more pleased, too.

QUESTIONS TO CONSIDER

1. Think of a time in the past year when you were a telephone customer. Did you have a good experience? What made it a good or a bad experience?

2. Do you think people are born with "good people skills," or do you think they acquire these skills? Do people also acquire listening skills, or are listening skills automatic?

3. How do you feel about being put on "hold" for a moment that turns into five minutes? Are there other things that irritate you when you are a telephone customer?

4. When you are on the telephone with someone, how long does it take you to detect whether that person is in a cheerful mood? How long does it take you to detect a bad attitude from the other person during a telephone conversation? Are there ways you recommend to avoid this negative situation?

5. Assume you have been given a script to use with callers. Are you able to use the script as it is written, or do you make changes depending on your mood or a caller's situation?

Delegation
What Are the Benefits of Delegating?

Some people think delegation is time-consuming and more trouble than doing a task or project themselves. Other people have experienced the benefits of delegation and they have discovered that it is an effective way to accomplish tasks and projects. Check out what you know about delegation by completing the following assessment.

Instructions   All of the following statements about the benefits of delegation are true *except one*. Circle the number of the statement below that is *not* true.

1. Delegating is a way to meet deadlines when you have too much to do.
2. Delegating is a way to get routine tasks accomplished by others.
3. Delegating is a way to obtain the expertise of someone else on a project.
4. Delegating is a way to get more people involved and committed to a project.
5. Delegating is a way to expand the skills of other workers.
6. Delegating is a way to bring fresh new ideas into a project.
7. Delegating is a way to manage a large number of projects simultaneously.
8. Delegating is a way to keep other people busy so they go on fewer breaks.
9. Delegating is a way to recognize the talents, interests, and enthusiasm of others.
10. Delegating is a way to create time for tasks and projects you prefer to do.
11. Delegating is a way to assign work and responsibility to others.
12. Delegating is a way to increase others' accountability for results.

SCORING AND INTERPRETATION

You should have circled number 8. It is the false statement, and all the remaining statements are true. Delegation is not intended to be a way to dump work on other people as punishment. If you thought more of the answers were false, you can benefit from a training program in which you discover what effective delegation is and is not.

QUESTIONS TO CONSIDER

1. Make a list of three work projects you could delegate right now. Add to the list two home projects you could delegate right now. Why are you keeping these projects for yourself?

2. Time is your most valuable resource at work. It takes time to delegate tasks and projects. Does it take less time to properly delegate or less time to do the tasks and projects yourself?

3. Trust is an important aspect of delegation. What experiences have you had with delegation when trust became a problem? For example, did someone else take the credit you deserved, or did someone delegate work to you and then abandon you to figure things out by yourself.

4. Successful delegation involves the sharing of information, not the dumping of projects and tasks. Have you had experiences to illustrate either of these two concepts? What were they?

5. Delegating projects to others increases their competence and commitment. What do you recall about a significant project that was delegated to you by a supervisor? In what ways did this project influence your views about delegating projects?

E-Mail
What Do You Need to Learn About Writing and Managing E-Mail?

E-mail is now an established form of business communication. It is fast, efficient, and effective. It requires the correct use of grammar and proper business writing, along with efficiency techniques and what has become "e-mail etiquette." Check your own knowledge by completing the following assessment.

Instructions   The following items are either "true" or "false." Mark your choice with T (true) or F (false) on the line preceding each of the items.

_____ 1. Proper grammar and punctuation are not relevant in e-mail messages of only two or three sentences.

_____ 2. Important e-mail messages should be written in all uppercase letters.

_____ 3. Exclamation points add credibility to your writing, so use them often.

_____ 4. Formatting an e-mail message is the same as formatting a message on paper.

_____ 5. Brief (one to two sentence) e-mail messages don't require proofreading.

_____ 6. When using numbers in e-mail messages, write out numbers between one and nine.

_____ 7. Avoid sending e-mail attachments when you can get along with a short message.

_____ 8. E-mail messages are more private and secure than paper messages.

_____ 9. There is no way to convey emotion in e-mail messages.

_____ 10. *Blind carbon copy* (BCC) means someone must read the message aloud to an unsighted person.

_____ 11. Long sentences indicate to your readers that you have superior intelligence.

_____ 12. Electronic junk mail can be deleted at work without opening it.

_____ 13. Include humor in all your e-mail messages.

_____ 14. Use as few words as possible for subject lines in e-mail.

_____ 15. Use key words in a subject line to help your reader keep track of your document.

SCORING AND INTERPRETATION

Instructions   The correct answers are as follows. Circle any you did not answer correctly.

1   F   Proper grammar and punctuation are always necessary.

2   F   Writing e-mail in uppercase letters is considered SHOUTING.

3   F   Use exclamation points sparingly. Overuse dilutes their impact and your credibility.

4   F   There is a new way of formatting. You will be learning more about it.

5   F   All messages require proofreading to eliminate grammatical or spelling errors.

6   F   In an e-mail message, you do not need to spell out numbers from 1 through 9.

7   T   Avoid attachments when you can send a brief message that includes the information.

8   F   E-mail messages are not secure, and they are no more secure than paper messages.

9   F   People are using what are often called "emoticons" to express an emotion, such as :-) to indicate a smile or :-(to indicate a frown.

10   F   Checking the BCC means that you are sending a copy to someone, but that others who receive the e-mail do not know this.

11   F   There is no scientific correlation between writing long sentences and superior intelligence.

12   T   To save your valuable time, delete as much junk mail as possible.

13   F   Using humor in business e-mail is tricky. Usually it is best to avoid it.

14   T   Be as specific and as brief as possible.

15   T   Sorting and storing e-mail is helped by the use of key words.

Congratulations if you missed only one of the items. Your readers appreciate your well-written e-mail messages. Keep up the good work.

If you missed two to four of the items, your e-mail messages will improve from attending a class on the topic. Your readers will be glad when you take the class.

If you missed more than five of the items, your e-mail messages are probably not being read with as much enthusiasm as you would like. After the class, your style of writing e-mail messages will change. Expect people to notice and appreciate the changes you make.

QUESTIONS TO CONSIDER

1. If everyone else at your workplace sends e-mail messages with incorrect spelling, bad grammar, and incomplete sentences, why should your messages be different?

2. Computers have changed the business landscape in a short time. What other changes in business communication methods have you experienced since you started working?

3. People at work are receiving information from a variety of sources. How many sources of information do you use? How many new pieces of information do you estimate you receive on an average workday?

4. It has been said that people should not use e-mail to send bad news to others. What are your feelings on this?

5. E-mail should be private. What are your thoughts about privacy in the workplace?

Ergonomics
What Makes Ergonomic Sense at Your Computer?

Ergonomics is the science of how you relate physically to your tasks and the equipment you use. Staying healthy while you work with computers is easy if you develop good habits and take the right precautions. Check out what you know about proper ergonomics by completing the following assessment.

Instructions   The following statements are either "true" (T) or "false" (F). Mark your choice on the line beside each statement.

_____ 1. If your fingers are above your wrists when you type, you should lower your keyboard or raise your chair.

_____ 2. You should create and use macros to save hundreds of keystrokes each day.

_____ 3. Using your mouse "properly" means that it is at keyboard height and within easy reach.

_____ 4. Using a mouse is generally safer for your wrists than using keyboard operations.

_____ 5. The top of your monitor screen should be slightly below your eye level and tilted upward.

_____ 6. When sitting, put a small cushion behind the small of your back to help maintain good posture.

_____ 7. Keep your feet on the floor.

_____ 8. Keep most of your weight on your seat.

_____ 9. Periodically drop your arms to your sides and shake out your wrists.

_____ 10. Avoid leaning on your elbows because it throws off your posture.

_____ 11. Get out of your chair and take a walk or move around for ten minutes every hour.

_____ 12. If you cannot vary your tasks, vary your positions.

_____ 13. Yawning is a good way to increase your oxygen intake and relax your eyes.

_____ 14. Lighting is best placed to your left or right so that glare is directed away from you.

_____ 15. The best place to put your computer is in front of a window.

SCORING AND INTERPRETATION

The last item (number 15) is the only one above that is false. (Experts say it is not a good idea to look into the bright background while working at your computer. It is also not a good idea to have the light from a window bouncing off your computer screen.) All the other statements are true. Are you surprised?

If you missed zero to three items, you have good ergonomic habits most of the time. Unfortunately, most of us know what to do but we do not routinely do the right things. It is important to maintain good ergonomic habits at all times.

If you missed more than four items, you must learn and practice safe work habits as soon as possible. You are on the path to serious and painful work injuries that you can prevent with new habits. A special training session will give you plenty of new ideas to create a safer work environment.

QUESTIONS TO CONSIDER

1. Your job title may not be computer operator, but if you spend over an hour a day at a computer you must practice safe work habits. Assuming that cost is not a problem, can you think of three items to purchase to make your work area more ergonomically correct?

2. Some people think it is important to have a chair that fits the person. What is your experience with this idea?

3. When you take your hourly ten-minute break to get out of your chair and move around to stay healthy, how do you explain this to people who accuse you of not working hard enough?

4. It is unnecessary to spend a fortune on the latest correct furniture and equipment. There are small, inexpensive items you can purchase or arrange for ergonomic safety. What have you seen people do successfully?

5. Can you demonstrate three exercises that you could do in your chair that could help increase your productivity?

Facilitation Skills
What Skills Do Effective Facilitators Practice?

Facilitation is used to help teams achieve their desired outcomes through productive dialogue. Often trainers or meeting leaders use facilitation skills to help people improve ways they identify and solve problems, make decisions, and deal with conflict. Facilitators have special skills that are not the same as the skills of trainers and presenters. Check out what you know about facilitation skills by taking the following assessment.

Instructions   For each of the following statements, mark whether you "agree" (A) or "disagree" (D) on the line provided.

_____ 1. The most important skill for facilitators is their ability to ask good questions.

_____ 2. Facilitators plan many questions in advance of a meeting.

_____ 3. Facilitators know that specific questions obtain better results.

_____ 4. One responsibility of a facilitator is to gain involvement and participation from all group members.

_____ 5. A facilitator provides a structure and methods to move a group toward consensus.

_____ 6. To encourage discussion, facilitators are expected to arrange appropriate seating and other aspects of the physical environment for a meeting.

_____ 7. When beginning discussion on a topic, facilitators ask a question of the entire group, rather than direct it to any individual.

_____ 8. Facilitators avoid asking questions that can be answered with a response of "yes" or "no," which may limit discussion.

_____ 9. Facilitators say, "That's a good question" and "That's a good idea" to encourage more people to offer their comments.

_____ 10. Facilitators ask many clarifying questions such as, "Who can summarize the group's position?"

_____ 11. Facilitators carefully monitor their own body language to avoid appearing to disapprove of something that would discourage discussion.

SCORING AND INTERPRETATION

If you marked all items A for "agree," you know a lot about facilitation skills. In the upcoming group discussion you are likely to have opportunities to share your experiences.

If you marked any items D for "disagree," you will be learning about how facilitators are more than discussion leaders, presenters, and trainers. Be sure to clarify the answers to any questions you may have with your trainer.

QUESTIONS TO CONSIDER

1. What experiences have you had as a member of a facilitated group? Were your experiences positive or negative? What made them that way?

2. Effective facilitators juggle many responsibilities simultaneously. Can you name three of these responsibilities?

3. It has been said that effective facilitators plan and manipulate as many details as they possibly can about the meeting place, agenda, meeting materials, and so forth. Why do you think this is true or not true?

4. Facilitators can expect to have difficult participants in some of their meetings. These people may behave in ways that negatively impact other participants. Because a facilitator's role is not to scold anyone, can you describe two other ways that he or she might choose to handle a difficult participant?

5. Often a facilitator asks a participant to record information generated by the group. What helpful information can the facilitator provide to the recorder to make this job more effective?

Geek Speak
Do You Know Geek Speak?

Computers have brought new terminology to the workplace. Another language has been added in the past few years, usually called "geek speak." Geek speak is the jargon and special vocabulary used by computer and information technology specialists, and it contains many familiar English words that have been given new meanings. As a person learns more about computers, the new terms become familiar. To find out how much geek speak you already understand, take the following short assessment.

Instructions   Match the following geek-speak terms with their meanings. Draw lines from one column to the other to connect the best matches.

Number	Term (Familiar Meaning)	Computer Terminology
1.	Virus (makes you sick)	Serial, parallel
2.	Memory (retained ideas)	Integrated circuit
3.	Interrupt (break into a conversation)	Swap device
4.	Execute (to kill)	Computer screen
5.	Spool (holds thread)	Launch a program
6.	Chip (snack)	Makes computer sick
7.	Ports (where ships dock)	Data storage
8.	Floppy (limp)	System failure
9.	Backup (go in reverse)	Removable disk
10.	Monitor (observe)	Hardware or software handler
11.	Bugs (insects)	Programmer problems
12.	Crash (vehicle accident)	Copy data

SCORING AND INTERPRETATION

Instructions   The following are the correct answers. Circle each term you did *not* correctly match. Put your total number of incorrect items on the line below.

Number	Term (Familiar Meaning)	Computer Terminology
1.	Virus (makes you sick)	Makes computer sick
2.	Memory (retained ideas)	Data storage
3.	Interrupt (break into conversation)	Hardware or software handler
4.	Execute (to kill)	Launch a program
5.	Spool (holds thread)	Swap device
6.	Chip (snack)	Integrated circuit
7.	Ports (where ships dock)	Serial, parallel
8.	Floppy (limp)	Removable disk
9.	Backup (go in reverse)	Copy data
10.	Monitor (observe)	Computer screen
11.	Bugs (insects)	Programmer problems
12.	Crash (vehicle accident)	System failure

Number Incorrect: _____

If you had zero to two incorrect matches, you are able to talk about computers with people who know computers and computer terminology. Most people learn these terms as they spend more time with their computers and with people who know about computers. Do you use geek speak routinely? If so, you may not be clearly understood by others who are unfamiliar with the new terminology.

If you had three to six incorrect matches, you are somewhat familiar with computer terminology, and your computer vocabulary will increase. When you see or hear a term that is unclear, learn its meaning. It will help your understanding of computer use.

If you had more than six incorrect matches, you are probably new to computer use. So many new terms may seem overwhelming at first. Like learning any other language, the secret is practice, practice, practice.

QUESTIONS TO CONSIDER

1. In addition to computers, can you think of other discoveries and inventions that have dramatically changed people's daily lives?

2. Some people thought they were finished learning new languages when they finished going to school. "Lifelong learning" is a new idea for many people. What do you think of the idea of lifelong learning?

3. In what ways do you believe technology will change your job in the next five years?

4. In what ways do you believe technology will change your life at home in the next five years? What technological skills do people learn and use at home that they will bring to their jobs?

5. For purposes of discussion, pretend computers do not exist. Describe your job in a world that never heard of computers. What do you do each day at work? How do you accomplish your tasks and responsibilities?

Goal Setting
Can You List the Steps for Setting a Goal?

The reason most people do not achieve their goals is that they never set any goals in the first place. They fail by default. You can avoid this by following a structured goal-setting strategy to achieve your goals. Successful people know where they are going, why they are going there, and how long it will take. Find out what you know about goal setting by completing the following assessment.

Instructions   The following eleven steps for setting goals are not in the correct sequence. Number the steps in their proper sequence on the lines provided. Numbers 4 and 10 are provided for you.

_____   Write down the goal in specific detail.

_____   Determine a reward for achieving the goal.

_____   Identify the goal.

_4_   Examine your commitment to the goal.

_____   Determine that the goal is realistic.

_____   Brainstorm a list of obstacles to reaching the goal.

_____   Make a detailed plan of action.

_10_   Brainstorm a list of benefits from achieving the goal.

_____   Identify people and resources to help reach the goal.

_____   Check that it is only one goal, not multiple goals.

_____   Set a deadline for achieving the goal.

SCORING AND INTERPRETATION

An eleven-step goal-setting strategy is listed below in the sequence generally recommended by success strategists. You may have chosen a different sequence, and you will be discussing similarities and differences during your training session. You have probably noticed that people use different routes to reach the same destination.

1. Identify the goal.
2. Check that it is only one goal, not multiple goals.
3. Write down the goal in specific detail.
4. Examine your commitment to the goal.
5. Set a deadline for achieving the goal.
6. Determine that the goal is realistic.
7. Brainstorm a list of obstacles to reaching the goal.
8. Identify people and resources to help reach the goal.
9. Make a detailed plan of action.
10. Brainstorm a list of benefits from achieving the goal.
11. Determine a reward for achieving the goal.

QUESTIONS TO CONSIDER

1. What goal-setting strategy do you use? Could you help someone else implement a goal-setting strategy? Where do most people learn goal-setting strategies?

2. Do you have lifetime goals? What are some advantages of setting long-term goals?

3. What short-term career goals do you have or wish to have? In what ways are career goals and financial goals related?

4. Some people believe it is important to live life according to a plan. Some people believe it is important to live life as it comes, moment by moment. What are your ideas about this?

5. Is there a connection between setting goals and managing time for accomplishing your tasks at work? What is that connection?

Home Office

Is Your Home Office Safe and Functional?

A home office must be a safe and functional work space. Whether you work at home on occasional projects or your home is your main place of work, your health and productivity demand that you pay attention to the details of your work area. Check yours out now by completing this assessment.

Instructions Mark each of the items listed below either "OK" or "AR" (action required):

OK = This is fine now   AR = Action required

____ 1. The desk work area is comfortable and pleasant.

____ 2. The desk work area is ergonomically correct.

____ 3. The work area chairs are safe and appropriate.

____ 4. Heating, ventilation, and air conditioning are adequate and in good repair.

____ 5. There is adequate ventilation for electrical equipment.

____ 6. Lighting is adequate for the work to be done.

____ 7. Equipment and furnishings over five feet high are secured to prevent toppling.

____ 8. Books are stored appropriately.

____ 9. There is adequate storage for work materials.

____ 10. Floor covering poses no hazards to rolling furniture.

____ 11. Cords and cables are out of the way so no one can trip on them.

____ 12. There are two exits from the work area in case of fire.

____ 13. There is a smoke detector nearby and a charged fire extinguisher.

OK = This is fine now   AR = Action required

_____ 14. The work area is free from combustible materials.

_____ 15. Electrical cords, plugs, and outlets are in good condition.

SCORING AND INTERPRETATION

If you marked OK for each item, your home office is safe and functional. Schedule periodic checks of the area using the list above and make adjustments as necessary. If you marked any items AR, it is time to make necessary changes.

QUESTIONS TO CONSIDER

1. Most people with home offices today did not grow up in homes with an office. They are strongly tempted to either purchase expensive new office furnishings or to use an assortment of discarded furnishings. What are your expectations about your home office?

2. Why is it important to discuss your work habits and work style preferences with others in your household?

3. Will other household members use your home office? If so, what rules will you impose?

4. What can you do to have enough outside social interaction if you work at home most of the time?

5. Successful home workers usually establish a routine about times to work, times for breaks and meals, work attire, and so forth. What routines do you follow?

Humor
Ready for Your Humor Checkup?

People who use their good sense of humor at work usually get along well with their co-workers. People who are overly stressed and have lost their good cheer can be frustrating to be around. They may also be bad for business because their irritability is contagious and turns away customers. However, it is important to use humor that will not offend others, and some types of humor are inappropriate in the workplace. Check your own use of humor in the workplace by completing the following assessment.

Instructions Think about your experiences at work during the past week and rate your use of humor according to the following scale:

1 = Never   2 = Seldom   3 = Sometimes   4 = Often   5 = Nearly always

____ 1. I maintained a good sense of humor at work during the past week.

____ 2. I smiled and acted in an upbeat manner.

____ 3. I shared appropriate laughs with coworkers.

____ 4. I am aware of what is fun and funny for my coworkers.

____ 5. I honored the difference between laughing *with* someone and laughing *at* someone.

____ 6. I was sensitive to the idea that not everyone laughs at the same things.

____ 7. I looked for ways to help lighten up my workdays.

____ 8. I added something cheerful or uplifting to my work environment.

____ 9. I looked for a silly way to solve a problem, and it helped me find a good solution.

____ 10. I shared some funny cartoons, stories, jokes, and so forth with coworkers.

1 = Never   2 = Seldom   3 = Sometimes   4 = Often   5 = Nearly always

____ 11. I refused to lose my sense of humor no matter what happened.

____ 12. I let something funny change my frustration and anger into laughter.

____ 13. I used a "begin work" ritual that started my days in a positive way.

____ 14. I used a silly "stop work" ritual that ended my work days and signaled time to stop working.

Total: _____

SCORING AND INTERPRETATION

Instructions   Total your responses and put your total on the line after "total" above.

If your total score is 50 to 70, you use your sense of humor at work. It probably helps you keep your stress level low and job satisfaction level high. You are probably well-liked by coworkers. As long as you are considerate of others' needs, your sense of humor helps everyone at work.

If your total score is 35 to 49, your sense of humor comes to work, but not often. Challenge yourself to add one way to lighten up your work day tomorrow and share it with coworkers.

If your total score is below 35, you probably believe laughter and fun do not mix with work. It is worth remembering that exercising your sense of humor is a way to gain friendship and support from others, as well as to enjoy life to the fullest.

QUESTIONS TO CONSIDER

1. Researchers tell us that fun breaks up conflict and tension at work. Can you recall experiences of this happening at your present job?

2. "Laughter is the best medicine." Do you agree or disagree with that statement? Why?

3. What are five appropriate ways to lighten up your work environment?

4. Some people believe laughter at work is unprofessional. What are your views? What ways do you recommend for stopping a coworker who uses inappropriate humor at work?

5. What are three suggestions you have to add appropriate humor to a meeting?

Information Overload

Are You on Information Overload?

During a typical workday you may send and receive up to two hundred messages and documents from a variety of sources. This is an overwhelming amount of data to manage unless you have (and use) procedures to handle it. Check whether you are on information overload by completing this assessment.

Instructions   The following list consists of tips for managing incoming information. For each item, make a check mark in the column that best describes your current situation.

I Do This Well	I Need to Improve	
_____	_____	1. I keep one main "To Do" list.
_____	_____	2. I streamline the number of places that I keep incoming information.
_____	_____	3. I use the same principles for organizing both paper and electronic information.
_____	_____	4. I coordinate my electronic filing system with my paper filing system.
_____	_____	5. I sort and file electronic and paper documents regularly.
_____	_____	6. I back up my electronic information on a regular basis.
_____	_____	7. I focus on information that is most important and avoid the remaining information.
_____	_____	8. I have faced the fact that I will never catch up.
_____	_____	9. I set realistic goals for myself about managing incoming information.

I Do This Well	I Need to Improve	
_____	_____	10. I toss out print materials and keep only bits of information that are important.
_____	_____	11. I schedule specific times on a regular basis to organize and to stay organized.
_____	_____	12. I eliminate duplication of information, such as watching three different morning news programs.
_____	_____	13. I schedule regular time to read work materials.
_____	_____	14. I skim written materials for what is important to me.
_____	_____	15. I discard unnecessary incoming information immediately.
_____	_____	16. I use a filing system that makes sense to me.

SCORING AND INTERPRETATION

Instructions   Look at your marks in the "I need to improve" column. These indicate areas in which you need to improve your information management skills. Prioritize these. Focus on your top priorities as you learn useful ways to reduce your stress and increase your effectiveness by managing incoming information. Many people believe they need to improve six or more of the listed areas. How did you do in comparison?

QUESTIONS TO CONSIDER

1. How do you think most people learn to manage new information? What do you notice is happening with information in the workplace today?

2. Think about a person you know who appears to manage incoming information well. What does this person do? What is one thing you could use from his or her system starting tomorrow?

3. Most people hate to think they will never catch up. What are your opinions about the inability to catch up?

4. In ten years do you think that information overload will be more or less a problem than it is today? What will happen to make this true?

5. From the experiences and frustrations you now have with information overload, what advice would you give to a person starting a first job?

Interruptions
How Do You Handle Interruptions at Work?

People complain about interruptions at work that keep them from completing their jobs. Some interruptions are part of job duties and responsibilities. Other regular interruptions interfere with productivity. There are ways to reduce unwanted and unnecessary interruptions. You may have discovered some of them for yourself. Check your effectiveness at handling interruptions by completing this assessment.

Instructions   Read each of the following statements and then rate your skills for handling interruptions at work by indicating whether you already do this well (DW) or whether you need practice (NP).

DW = Do Well   NP = Need Practice

_____ 1. When I am busy and I receive a personal phone call, I say I'm busy and I will call back later unless the matter is urgent.

_____ 2. I set "telephone hours" when others can expect to reach me each day.

_____ 3. I let my calls go to voice mail when I am in the middle of something important.

_____ 4. When someone asks to speak with me I say something like, "I can speak with you in five minutes if that is all right."

_____ 5. I ask someone else to handle my calls or customers when I must handle an urgent and important matter immediately.

_____ 6. I set aside time each day or each week when I am not to be interrupted.

_____ 7. I close my door to minimize interruptions from people walking in.

_____ 8. When someone interrupts me when I am busy, I immediately stand up and stay standing to convey the idea that I will soon sit down and return to the work I was doing.

DW = Do Well   NP = Need Practice

____ 9. I say to interrupters, "I only have four minutes. Will that be enough time for this?"

____ 10. I use a "Do Not Disturb" sign on occasion.

____ 11. I tell interrupters I have a deadline and must return to work.

____ 12. I tell interrupters, "I'm very busy and I can't talk now. Perhaps next time."

____ 13. My coworkers and I rotate times when we cover interruptions for one another.

____ 14. I tell people I prefer that they leave voice mail messages when possible.

Total DW Responses: _____

SCORING AND INTERPRETATION

Instructions   Count the number of DW responses you selected and put that number on the line following the statements. If the number is 10 or more, congratulations. You are doing a fine job of controlling the majority of interruptions that reduce your productivity at work. Still, you may feel you would like to learn more ways to handle interruptions.

If your DW number is 6 or under, you are probably frustrated about the interruptions you receive at work every day. You will learn techniques in this training session to help you handle the interruptions better. This will cut down on your frustration and help you manage your work more effectively.

QUESTIONS TO CONSIDER

1. Some people believe it is rude to tell someone else you only have four minutes to talk. Do you believe this is rude behavior at work? Is it rude behavior at home? Is it rude behavior with your friends?

2. In the old days people were only interrupted when someone came to them or called out to them. Today, in addition to those ways, we have added telephones, pagers, voice mail, e-mail, and a variety of notification systems on computers. There are many more ways to interrupt people than before. What is your opinion about this trend?

3. Assume that you have suggested a good method for handling interruptions to someone else. The person says, "I tried that once and it didn't work." What will you say next?

4. How do you feel about handling interruptions from your boss? Assume for a moment that your boss is one of the worst interrupters at work. What ideas do you have for getting back to work quickly after such an interruption?

5. What can you say to people when *you* are the interrupter? Are there ways you can minimize your own tendency to interrupt others?

Job Satisfaction
Are You Satisfied with Your Job?

Compared with a hundred years ago, people today have increased education and mobility and choices in how they earn a living. Still, a large percentage of working adults express dissatisfaction with their jobs and career fields. How satisfied are you with your job? Find out by taking the following assessment.

Instructions For each statement below mark your selection on the line provided.

A = Agree D = Disagree

____ 1. My job is okay but it isn't "me."

____ 2. I would like my job better if I could rearrange my work area.

____ 3. I thought that I would have a better job by this time in my life.

____ 4. My job would be better if I had a more understanding boss.

____ 5. I think I need to explore other types of work.

____ 6. My job would be better if there were fewer distractions.

____ 7. If I receive a promotion I'll be happier at work.

____ 8. My job would be better if my boss had better management skills.

____ 9. I fell into this kind of work and I would rather be doing something else.

____ 10. I prefer either a quieter or a more exciting place to work.

____ 11. I worry that I won't have enough retirement income from this job.

____ 12. I want a manager who appreciates the efforts I make.

____ 13. My job under-uses my talents, interests, and abilities.

A = Agree   D = Disagree

____ 14. I would be more productive if I had different equipment to work with.

____ 15. By this point in my current job, I had expected that work days would be easier and go by quickly.

____ 16. I would like to have coworkers who share some of my interests.

SCORING AND INTERPRETATION

Instructions   How many "A" (agree) responses did you mark for the following items? Place the numbers in the blanks below.

(CP)   Numbers 1, 5, 9, 13 = _____
(WE)   Numbers 2, 6, 10, 14 = _____
(CE)   Numbers 3, 7, 11, 15 = _____
(MP)   Numbers 4, 8, 12, 16 = _____

Each of the question sets above focused on a different aspect of your job. The more "A" responses you had within a set, the more likely that your dissatisfaction with your job is centered in a particular area. If you had zero to two "A" responses in an area, this is not a major cause of job dissatisfaction for you at this time.

Your CP score is your *career planning* score. If you have a 3 or 4 on this line, it indicates you could benefit from consulting a career counselor. You may decide to go through a series of assessments and research activities to select a different career. A career counselor will help you set goals to make changes in your work life.

Your WE score is your *work environment* score. If you have a 3 or 4 on this line, it indicates your dissatisfaction with your work environment. Identify the specific environmental aspects that are most unpleasant for you and that interfere with your productivity. Select two of these to discuss with your supervisor. Your productivity will increase when you make needed changes in your work environment.

Your CE score is your *career expectation* score. If you have a 3 or 4 on this line, it indicates that your present work situation is not what you expected for yourself at your age and the present stage of your life. You are probably disappointed in what you have accomplished so far. You may want to consult with a career counselor who will help you to identify new goals and make action plans to achieve them.

Your MP score is your *management/people* score. If you have a 3 or 4 on this line, it indicates your dissatisfaction with your manager and other people you work around. You may want to be around different people, perhaps those who share your personal interests and important work values. Focus on this aspect of your work life and describe the people who could contribute to your increased job satisfaction. Find ways to bring these people into your life on or off your job.

QUESTIONS TO CONSIDER

1. Most adults have done little career planning after high school. Because the work world has changed so dramatically in the past twenty years, why might career planning be a good idea for adults?

2. For some people it is nonsense to complain about their work environment. They say, "It is what it is, and only the boss can change it." Yet it is a well-known fact that our surroundings influence our mood and our productivity. How would you advise someone who wants to make changes in the work environment, such as noise control, different colors on walls, different lighting, new furniture arrangements, or other elements of his or her work environment?

3. Assuming that work is important to you, but that your work is not your entire life, how do you know when to adjust your career expectations to present realities? How do you know which battles to fight? What long-range plans do you have to maintain a balanced life?

4. What ideas do you have about being a supervisor or manager during your career? What positive experiences have you had with your supervisors and managers? Describe the influence a supervisor or manager has on a person's career.

5. What are your ideas about balancing work life and the rest of life? Do you have tips to help others do this better? What is the connection between job satisfaction and a balanced life?

Job Search

Do You Have Up-to-Date Job Search Skills?

People look for jobs in a variety of ways. What is effective at one time may not be as effective at another time. When looking for a job, it is important to do as many activities as you can each day to keep up the momentum of your job search. The following assessment is intended to help you focus your search for a job.

Instructions   For each of the job search tasks listed below, mark on the line in front of each statement how you are progressing.

D = Doing Well   I = Improvement Needed

____   1.   I use networking skills to tap into the "hidden job market."

____   2.   I am looking for a job using the Internet.

____   3.   I plan meetings to discuss my job skills and prospects with at least two people each day.

____   4.   I take classes to learn the latest computer skills.

____   5.   I take classes to develop my writing skills.

____   6.   I take classes to develop my public speaking skills.

____   7.   I follow my career plan to guide my job search activities.

____   8.   I use my job search plan to guide my daily activities.

____   9.   Looking for a job is my job right now and I stick with it.

____   10.   I take weekends off from my job search just as I did from my job.

____   11.   My friends are supportive and helpful and I ask for what I need.

____   12.   My family is aware of my job seeking activities. They are supportive.

D = Doing Well   I = Improvement Needed

____ 13. I use my expanding network of contacts to help me with seeking a job.

____ 14. I have a great resume and I am comfortable using it.

____ 15. I write great cover letters for my resume.

____ 16. I always send a cover letter with my faxed resume.

____ 17. I always send thank-you letters for interviews and favors.

____ 18. I can brag appropriately about my accomplishments any time, any place.

____ 19. I do a lot of interviewing for information and research purposes.

____ 20. I have been doing practice job interviews with someone I trust.

Total D Responses: _____   Total I Responses: _____

SCORING AND INTERPRETATION

Instructions   Total your D responses and put your total on the line following the statements. Total your I responses and put your total on the line provided.

Is your D total higher than your I total? If it is, you are taking many of the right action steps to find and obtain your next job. If you have marked any statements with an I, look back at these and select one to work on all of the following week. It may help if you schedule time with a friend or a career counselor to discuss your job search.

QUESTIONS TO CONSIDER

1. Employers today are looking for people with a broad range of skills. What happens if you have excellent job skills and poor sales skills? What happens if you have excellent job skills and poor interpersonal skills?

2. What do you recommend to people who say they are too old or too young to find a good job?

3. Can you describe a job interview in general terms? What makes a job interview successful?

4. "If you have any problem areas you prefer not to discuss during job interviews, figure out in advance how you will address these areas." What does this statement mean to you?

5. What are your ideas about a job seeker who has several resumes? How could you use different resumes?

     Assessments A to Z/© 2000 Jossey-Bass/Pfeiffer

Keynote Speaking Skills

Are You Ready to Be a Keynote Speaker?

Keynote speeches are often a main focus of meetings and conferences. You could be asked to be a keynote speaker. Are you ready? Check by taking the following assessment.

Instructions   Assume that you have been asked to give a keynote speech at an important company event two months from now. Read each of the following statements and determine whether it is true (T) or false (F).

____ 1. They asked you to be the speaker, which means that you are expected to tell the audience everything there is to know about your topic.

____ 2. Because nearly everyone in the company knows you, it is appropriate to give an impromptu speech instead of a planned speech.

____ 3. You should write your own introduction and give it to the person who will be introducing you as soon as you can.

____ 4. Before you begin your speech, tap the microphone three or four times to be sure it is working at the right level for you.

____ 5. You must begin a keynote speech with a joke or funny story to make the audience laugh.

____ 6. If you decide to use slides, use them from the beginning to the end of your speech at the rate of about one per minute.

____ 7. Keynote speeches always take longer than planned, so there is no reason to be concerned about the length of your speech.

_____ 8. If you usually become nervous and have stage fright, eat a big meal before your speech.

_____ 9. It is a good idea to tell the audience a story about something that happened to you that is related to the topic.

_____ 10. Keynote speakers must use visuals, such as slides and overheads.

_____ 11. Keynote speakers must never move around in the audience.

_____ 12. If you use a conversational tone for your speech, your audience will connect with you better.

_____ 13. If you plan to use notes, be sure the audience does not see you using them.

_____ 14. You can use a long, unexpected pause to change the rhythm of your speech and jolt your audience to attention.

_____ 15. At the end of your speech, thank the audience for being so kind and for listening to you.

SCORING AND INTERPRETATION

The following items are true: 3, 9, 12, and 14. The following items are false, and brief explanations are provided.

1. They asked you to be the keynote speaker so you would talk about some part of your expertise, most likely a part of your knowledge that will be of special interest to their own work situations. You must force yourself to limit your topic.

2. Avoid confusing *impromptu* with *informal*. You may deliver an informal speech, but you will take several hours to plan and prepare for it thoroughly.

4. Never tap the microphone for any reason. Tapping is the action of an amateur; it produces sounds that annoy your audience.

5. You must begin your keynote speech with an attention-grabbing device. It could be a joke or funny story, a question, a starting fact, or another device you will learn about in your class.

6. When you use slides, avoid "slideswiping" your audience by showing one slide after another throughout your presentation. Use slides sparingly, and use them for impact.

7. Professional keynote speakers know they may be asked to shorten their speeches to keep the program on schedule. They are rarely asked to lengthen their speeches to fill time. Your program planners want you to keep to the requested schedule, so it is your job to plan accordingly and expect to be flexible.

8. Most professional speakers eat sparingly, if at all, before speaking. They have learned that their minds are more alert when their bodies are not digesting a lot of food.

10. Keynote speakers are responsible for getting their message across to their audience. This can involve using slides and overheads, or other types of visual aids. There is no rule that they must use visuals. However, visuals are powerful teaching and learning devices.

11. Moving around within the audience can be a powerful method for keynote speakers to get their message across to people. There is no rule that speakers must stand behind a lectern.

13. It is all right if your audience sees your speaker notes. It is not all right if they see you reading your notes.

15. Professional speakers and their coaches recommend that you finish your speech with a powerful statement, perhaps a quote or anecdote. When your powerful ending is over, stop. Wait for the applause. Smile at your audience.

If you missed zero to two answers, you could probably do a good job as a keynote speaker as long as you plan ahead and practice your speech.

If you missed three or more items, concentrate on improving your speaking skills and build your confidence to give a keynote speech at a later time.

QUESTIONS TO CONSIDER

1. Do you recall a speech you gave when you were a teenager? How confident did you feel? Did you enjoy any of your teen speaking experiences?

2. Think of a time you were impressed by a keynote speech. What did the speaker do that you liked?

3. How do people build their skills and confidence to give keynote speeches?

4. Do you think a speaker's appearance influences how readily an audience accepts the speaker's message? Can you think of examples to support your beliefs?

5. If you could earn $1 million for giving a keynote speech next week, what topic would you select? Why did you select that topic? Who would you ask to help you prepare?

Assessments A to Z/© 2000 Jossey-Bass/Pfeiffer

Leadership
Is Leadership Lacking in Your Workplace?

Lack of leadership may cause a team or an organization to flounder. Often leaders believe they are providing good leadership when in fact they are not. The following list of workplace events contains indicators and symptoms of a lack of leadership. See whether these indicators exist in your workplace.

Instructions   Read the following statements and rate each on the following scale *as to whether they are true where you work*:

1 = not true   2 = rarely true   3 = sometimes true   4 = often true   5 = always true

____   1.   Workers make no suggestions for improvements.

____   2.   There are turf battles over resources and assignments.

____   3.   There are complaints after meetings about issues not discussed in the meetings.

____   4.   Workers have no pride in their organization or work.

____   5.   Relationships between coworkers are strained.

____   6.   Us-versus-them talk is heard often.

____   7.   Workers are unwilling to take responsibility for their mistakes.

____   8.   Worker complaints are increasing.

____   9.   Workers are complaining more about their working conditions.

____   10.   People are missing an increasing number of deadlines.

____   11.   There appears to be an increase in unethical behavior.

____   12.   The "program of the month" to fix things is a joke.

____   13.   Workers appear to want more information from their managers than is given.

1 = not true   2 = rarely true   3 = sometimes true   4 = often true   5 = always true

____ 14. Workers are asking for more involvement in decision making.

____ 15. It is increasingly difficult to find new, talented workers.

____ 16. Workers do not take on leadership roles, even when the opportunity presents itself.

____ 17. High-performing workers are leaving to work elsewhere.

____ 18. There is an overly active rumor mill.

____ 19. Workers act as though their assignments are a waste of their time.

Total: _____

SCORING AND INTERPRETATION

Instructions   Total your responses and place the number on the line above.

If your total is less than 60, you are probably experiencing good leadership where you work. You are most likely satisfied with your work situation and the way work is done in your organization.

If your total is 60 or above, people are experiencing the problems that accompany lack of strong leadership. The higher your score, the more challenges you encounter each day at work. Stronger leadership would eliminate many of the problems you and your coworkers experience.

QUESTIONS TO CONSIDER

1. As organizations become less hierarchical and flatter, leadership responsibilities are being spread around. How comfortable are you with this trend? What are ways you can increase your comfort level with this idea?

2. "Leaders are born, not made." What are your thoughts about this statement?

3. What experiences have you had that have made you a better leader?

4. There are many different ways of leading people. What ways can you think of?

5. Some workers are better at leading projects than at leading people, while other workers are better leaders of people than they are of projects. What are your experiences with this?

Assessments A to Z/© 2000 Jossey-Bass/Pfeiffer

Letter and Memo Writing

Is It Time to Check Your Writing Skills?

When you send letters and memos, electronically or otherwise, your recipients expect you to know how to write properly. Test your letter-writing knowledge by completing the following assessment.

Instructions   Circle the number of each item below that is *false*.

1. Use an *attention* line in a business letter only when the inside address does not include an individual or department name, and type it two lines under the address at the left margin.

2. Involve your reader with the use of "you" by beginning your sentences with the word "you" when possible, and then telling your readers what is in it for them to keep them reading.

3. When writing a business letter, state the main point at the beginning.

4. When you write a letter that contains bad news, it is a good idea to present good news first, as it gives the reader a reason to read beyond the beginning. If there is no positive news, begin with a friendly tone and end with a supportive statement.

5. Indenting the first line of each paragraph in a letter or memo is no longer standard; double spacing between paragraphs is standard.

6. If your letter or memo is longer than one page, make sure that the second page contains at least three or four lines.

7. When you include more than one attachment to a memo or letter, put the number of attachments in parentheses after the word "Attachments."

8. When you are writing technical or difficult material, short paragraphs are more reader-friendly. A good paragraph length is six lines.

9. Sentences with more than twenty words are too long to be easily followed.

10. The equally spaced periods that fill in for missing words, called ellipses, can contain as many periods as you wish.

11. When finishing a letter, say what you would say in person to end a conversation, such as, "Let me know if you need more information."

12. Use exclamation points sparingly, if at all, and let your words convey your meaning.

13. The correct way to write percentages is to give percentages in figures and write out the word percent, as in "74 percent."

14. Periods always go inside quotation marks.

SCORING AND INTERPRETATION

Item 10 is the only false item. The others are true. If you circled *only* item number 10, congratulations. Your letter-writing skills are excellent. Did you know that ellipses always have *three* periods when written correctly?

If you circled three or more items, you will benefit from an update of your letter-writing skills. You may also want to check a business-writing book or online writing guide before sending your letters until you are confident about your skills.

If you circled more than five items, you may want to ask someone who is a good writer to coach you with your letter writing for a few weeks. A class in business letter writing will increase your skills and confidence.

QUESTIONS TO CONSIDER

1. You have probably heard the statement, "We only have one chance to make a first impression." How does this statement relate to letter writing?

2. Rules of grammar and standard business procedure have changed over the years. What is one thing you learned in school that has now changed?

3. Some people think it is "cheating" to consult a business-writing guide to make letters better. What are your thoughts on this?

4. If your boss wants you to write something in a way that you know is not correct or is not the modern way, how will you handle this situation?

5. If your workplace has a style guide for you to use when writing letters, and there is information in it that contradicts what you have recently learned, how would you handle this?

Assessments A to Z/© 2000 Jossey-Bass/Pfeiffer

Listening Skills
How Do You Rate Your Listening Skills?

Have you ever felt as though someone was not listening to you? Have you ever been accused of not listening to someone else? Listening is not easy. Listening is a skill that people can learn at any time and improve throughout their lives. Check your skills on the following assessment.

Instructions   Each of the following items represents an aspect of effective listening. Think about a difficult situation you experienced with someone at work during the past two weeks. Thinking about this difficult experience, rate yourself according to the following scale. Put your response on the line in front of each item.

1 = None of the time   2 = Rarely   3 = About half the time   4 = Most of the time   5 = All of the time

____   1.   I faced the person throughout the conversation.

____   2.   I did not interrupt.

____   3.   I did not talk while the other person was speaking.

____   4.   I listened for main ideas and concepts.

____   5.   I listened for vocal tones.

____   6.   I observed body language.

____   7.   I kept an open mind.

____   8.   I did not use the person's pauses as my signal to begin speaking.

____   9.   I used appropriate listening responses such as "I see."

____ 10.   I asked questions to clarify the speaker's meaning.

____ 11.   I did not plan what I was going to say while the person was speaking.

1 = None of the time   2 = Rarely   3 = About half the time   4 = Most of the time   5 = All of the time

____ 12. I maintained appropriate body language.

____ 13. I maintained appropriate facial expressions.

____ 14. I maintained appropriate voice control.

____ 15. I did not use fake smiles.

Total: _____

SCORING AND INTERPRETATION

Instructions   Total your score and write it on the line above.

If your score is 60 to 75, you used excellent listening skills during the difficult situation you encountered. When you concentrate on listening, you do it well most of the time. Your coworkers and friends probably believe that you are a good listener.

If your score is 45 to 59, you can learn to listen more skillfully, especially in difficult situations with others. To begin improving your skills, choose one aspect of effective listening to concentrate on today.

If you scored below 45, the other person surely did not believe you were listening. Looking back at the fifteen items, can you choose two that were most difficult for you? For the rest of the week, focus on improving your skills in those areas.

QUESTIONS TO CONSIDER

1. What is the difference between hearing and listening? Do you think people generally listen more often or hear more often? Why is this?

2. How do you feel about people who really listen to you when you are happy? Sad? Angry? Complaining?

3. Some people believe there would be increased productivity at work if people listened to one another better. What do you think about that?

4. Do you know someone who is a good listener most of the time? How would you describe this person?

5. Can you think of a funny situation that happened to you or someone else because of poor listening skills? Was it funny at the time it happened? Why or why not?

Meetings
How Can You Have More Effective Meetings?

Meetings have been called the biggest time waster in the workplace. Bad meetings waste more than time, they waste money. Fortunately, people can learn new ideas that lead to more effective meeting management. Take the following assessment to discover what you have to learn about effective meetings.

Instructions   For each of the statements below mark T for "true" or F for "false."

____   1.   Effective meetings start and end on time.

____   2.   A meeting agenda should be given to everyone who is expected to attend a meeting.

____   3.   A meeting agenda should go out in advance of the meeting.

____   4.   People listed on the meeting agenda should be prepared for their topics.

____   5.   There is computer software that helps with meeting management.

____   6.   There are alternatives to many meetings.

____   7.   For a meeting to be effective it must last for a minimum of 30 minutes.

____   8.   When a meeting goes over the scheduled time, people are free to leave.

____   9.   A meeting is defined as a time when people gather and sit down and talk.

____   10.   It doesn't matter who attends a meeting as long as the team is well-represented.

____   11.   A good time to have a meeting is after lunch.

____   12.   Visual aids are for training, not for meetings.

SCORING AND INTERPRETATION

Items 1 through 6 are true and items 7 through 12 are false. You may have correctly answered every item, but knowing what to do and making it happen are two different things. Your challenge is to find a way to make the needed changes in meetings where you work.

If you missed any items, discuss your ideas with your trainer and fellow participants. Some workplaces have their own particular meetings procedures and customs, but that does not mean that they cannot be improved.

QUESTIONS TO CONSIDER

1. What must happen before people take meeting management at work more seriously?

2. Do you have any suggestions for ways to use technology to make meetings more effective?

3. What effective ways have you seen someone use to get people back on the topic at a meeting? Which of these ways could you experiment with during the next meeting you attend?

4. When a meeting is over, people leave. What else should they do?

5. It has been said that "meetings never get better because people keep doing the same things over and over." What is one suggestion you have to put a stop to this tendency?

Mentoring
What Do Mentors Do?

Mentoring can be an informal or a formal process. Many people use a mentor to learn technical skills and to achieve career goals. During your lifetime and your career you have probably been a mentor or a mentee many times. Fill out the following assessment to see how much you know about the process of mentoring.

Instructions   As you read the following list, recall instances when you were mentored and when you were a mentor for someone else. Mark one or both columns before each of the items below to reflect your personal experiences with mentoring.

Done for Me	I Have Done	
_____	_____	1. Assisted with career issues.
_____	_____	2. Identified strengths.
_____	_____	3. Identified weaknesses.
_____	_____	4. Shared personal experiences.
_____	_____	5. Offered encouragement.
_____	_____	6. Connected with resources.
_____	_____	7. Built self-confidence.
_____	_____	8. Coached professional behavior.
_____	_____	9. Offered friendship.
_____	_____	10. Provided reality tests for ideas.
_____	_____	11. Confronted negative attitudes.
_____	_____	12. Taught by good example.
_____	_____	13. Explained how things get done.

Done for Me	I Have Done	
_____	_____	14. Praised good performance.
_____	_____	15. Acted as public relations person.

SCORING AND INTERPRETATION

As you have probably noticed, people give and receive mentoring throughout their lives. Many people mark nearly every item on the list above. These people know there is a lot to be learned from others and are willing to offer their assistance to others as well.

QUESTIONS TO CONSIDER

1. How important is it that a mentor and a mentee like one another?

2. In formal mentoring programs the mentors and mentees are paired by a program coordinator. What are the advantages and disadvantages of this arrangement?

3. Name two benefits for a company of having a mentoring program. Name two benefits for the mentors.

4. How could a formal mentoring program help an organization that is having a problem finding good people to hire?

5. What do you believe is the most important personal characteristic of a good mentor?

Negotiation
Do You Know How to Negotiate for a Pay Increase?

People generally avoid talking about salary and asking for more money, so it's no wonder they avoid negotiating for pay increases. When you want more money and you believe you deserve more money, you can either wait for your boss to make you an offer or make your boss an offer. Which option is more effective? Take the following assessment to see what you know about negotiating for a salary increase.

Instructions   For each of the following statements mark on the line provided whether it is T (true) or F (false) for you.

_____ 1. I have researched what jobs like mine pay elsewhere.

_____ 2. I have facts and data to prove my value to my organization.

_____ 3. I know my value in the marketplace.

_____ 4. I know exactly what I want in the way of salary.

_____ 5. I know what non-monetary items I will trade for equivalent money.

_____ 6. I have studied up on negotiating skills.

_____ 7. I have considered the best time to schedule a meeting to discuss a pay increase.

_____ 8. I am willing to make a reasonable request.

_____ 9. I am willing to wait a reasonable time for a pay increase.

_____ 10. I will not make idle threats about leaving my job.

_____ 11. I know how to respond to the objections I expect to hear.

_____ 12. I have practiced for a meeting to discuss a pay increase.

SCORING AND INTERPRETATION

Did you mark T (true) for every item? Congratulations. You appear to be ready to arrange that important negotiation meeting. Any items not marked "true" indicate areas for you to work on before meeting with anyone to ask for a pay increase. You will greatly increase your chances for successfully negotiating a pay increase if you have done your homework and prepared yourself.

QUESTIONS TO CONSIDER

1. How do you explain the unwillingness of people to talk about their financial situations, especially salary, with others?

2. Many people research thoroughly before purchasing a vehicle and prepare to negotiate with a vehicle salesperson. Why don't people do that when they want a pay increase?

3. What ideas did you have when you were in your first job about how to obtain a pay raise?

4. Why is it not a good idea to discuss your personal needs during a meeting about a pay increase?

5. "They will give me what I deserve." What does this statement mean to you?

Networking
How Could You Use Networking for Job Advancement?

Networking is the process of establishing and maintaining relationships with others to exchange information and resources informally in ways that are mutually beneficial. Every day we have networking conversations with people around us, although we may not think of them as such. From our networking conversations we exchange information and resources to help both with our work lives and with the rest of our lives. Take the following assessment to see what you know about networking with others.

Instructions   All of the following statements are true except one. Find and circle the false statement.

1. There is more to networking than shaking hands and asking for people's business cards.

2. Identify people you want to network with, go where they go, and make an effort to meet them.

3. Locate the organizations of the people you want to meet and go there to meet people.

4. Volunteer for committees to increase your visibility in your key interest groups.

5. Write a compelling article or letter to an editor that people in your key interest groups are likely to read and comment about.

6. Become a master of making purposeful small talk.

7. Have a few prepared chit-chat topics to help you start a conversation when you meet others.

8. Avoid the appearance of being a salesperson of any type.

9. Learn to be an extraordinary listener.

10. Become proficient at remembering names.

11. Contact people regularly to ask how they can help you.

12. Use an electronic or paper system for organizing and storing networking information.

13. Do something meaningful with your networking database, such as sending people birthday cards, inviting them to meetings of mutual interest, and so forth.

14. Networking happens everywhere.

SCORING AND INTERPRETATION

Did you find the false item? Number 11 is false. This is, in fact, the reason networking has a bad reputation for some people. Networking is a two-way relationship. If you contact people regularly to ask for what *you* want, it appears to be a one-way relationship with the other person on the giving end and you on the receiving end. When you contact people, think of what you can offer to *them*.

QUESTIONS TO CONSIDER

1. Recall your earliest networking experiences. What were they like?

2. How did you meet your closest friend? Was there any networking involved? Did networking help you find your current job?

3. Think back to your first job. Was any networking involved in the experience?

4. Some people are born with outgoing personalities and they network naturally. For everyone else, networking is work—and may not be much fun. What ideas do you have to overcome the negative aspects?

5. "If you are a good person and work really hard and harm no one, you will receive all the good opportunities as your reward." What do you think of this statement?

Office Behavior
What Do You Know About Office Politics?

When someone says the words "office politics," it brings to mind negative rather than positive ideas for most people. Yet politics are a part of everyday life for each of us. We must learn to use positive politics at the office to get what we need. Some ideas are listed in the following assessment. See how many of them you practice.

Instructions   Each of the following statements may or may not be a way to become involved with *positive* politics at work. On the line provided, mark Y for "yes" if you think the statement is descriptive of positive politics or N for "no" if you think the statement is not descriptive of positive politics.

____   1.   I make it my business to know what my boss wants done.

____   2.   I meet everyone in my work area and allow them to know something about me.

____   3.   I know the value of my department to this organization.

____   4.   I would never let anyone at work see me lose my temper.

____   5.   It is important to keep my resume up-to-date at all times.

____   6.   I takes classes to help me write more effectively.

____   7.   I take classes to learn more about effective public speaking.

____   8.   I share my knowledge and talent with others at work.

____   9.   I learn new skills and I tell others what I have learned.

____   10.   I make sure I have an informal talk with my boss at least once every week.

____   11.   I have a social meal with my coworkers every two weeks or so.

____   12.   I belong to a professional organization for my occupation, and I urge others to join me at meetings.

_____ 13. I volunteer for interesting opportunities at work.

_____ 14. I plug into the grapevine as a listener only.

_____ 15. I make a point of meeting people in this organization who are outside my work area.

SCORING AND INTERPRETATION

Each statement above is an illustration of positive politics. Did you mark every statement with a Y? The statements are examples of what you can do to manage your own career successfully. If you are troubled by item number 5, remember that your boss could ask for your resume to consider putting you on an important committee. Or you may want to give your resume to someone for a different reason. It is not disloyal to keep your resume up-to-date.

QUESTIONS TO CONSIDER

1. Where did you first experience what you would call "office politics"? Was this a positive or negative experience for you?

2. Do you have any additional ideas of ways you can play positive politics at your job, other than those listed above?

3. What advice do you have for someone starting a new job on how to play positive politics?

4. Can you think of a response that would stop someone from telling you office gossip you did not wish to hear?

5. Learning to work well with people you don't like is part of playing positive politics. What are some of your ideas on how to do this?

Organizational Skills

Do You Know Enough About Organizing Your Work Space?

Organized work spaces don't happen because of magic. They are the result of plans and efforts to maintain those plans. Take the following assessment to discover how many helpful techniques and work habits you use to organize your work space.

Instructions   Rate yourself on each of the techniques and work habits listed below according to the following scale.

1 = Rarely or never   2 = Sometimes   3 = Almost always

____ 1. I clear off my work area at the end of each work day.

____ 2. I have a designated place for incoming materials and I use it.

____ 3. I have a designated place for unread mail and I use it.

____ 4. I have a designated place for professional material that I want to read later.

____ 5. I handle each piece of my incoming mail only once.

____ 6. I keep clutter off my work area.

____ 7. I have a system for managing my incoming e-mail messages and I use it.

____ 8. I use color coding to help with paper filing.

____ 9. I maintain a file that reminds me of important items for follow-up.

____ 10. I can find information from my files within two attempts.

____ 11. I have a daily "to do" list and I use it.

1 = Rarely or never   2 = Sometimes   3 = Almost always

____ 12. I have a list of current projects, and I consult it and update it.

____ 13. I clean out my files on a regular basis.

____ 14. I use a system for keeping track of contact information.

____ 15. My work space is neat and orderly at all times.

Total: _____

SCORING AND INTERPRETATION

Instructions   Total your responses and put your total on the line following the statements.

Although no one is perfect at all times, if your score is above 35 you appear to others to be well-organized. You know it takes some work to get that way and stay that way. You could probably teach your coworkers a few tips and tricks you have learned that will help them. Congratulations to you for having an organized work space and good organizing habits.

If your score is 29 to 34, you have some good organizing habits and ideas. You probably become too busy or distracted to do a better job of organizing your work space. You know being organized helps make your work life easier, so set aside time to make an organization plan.

If your score is below 29, you have difficulty keeping track of important information and events. You probably miss important dates. You likely spend time apologizing for your disorganization to your coworkers. The good news is that you can improve your situation by learning and practicing new skills immediately.

QUESTIONS TO CONSIDER

1. Where did you learn your ideas about organizing your work space? Did you ever work closely with someone who was very well-organized? What are two things this person did that you can copy tomorrow?

2. If you work with a disorganized person, does it impact your productivity?

3. Name two personal benefits of having your work space 98 percent organized.

4. Can you bring to your work space any organizing tips and tricks that you use at home? Are there organizing tools you use at home that can be used in the office, too?

5. What would happen if you went shopping for work space organizing ideas at a specialty store, office supply catalog, or online? What would happen if you discussed this shopping venture with your boss before you went shopping?

Problem Solving
Do You Know Twelve Steps for Problem Solving?

Twelve steps for problem solving can help you resolve most types of problems at work if you follow them in the proper order. They are listed out of order in the following assessment. See whether you can list them in the proper order.

Instructions The following twelve steps for problem solving are not in order. Put them in the best possible order by placing the correct number beside each item on the line provided. The first step is numbered for you.

_____ Know when to stop gathering data and ideas for making a decision.

_____ Eliminate the trivial and concentrate on the major issues.

_____ Make modifications as needed in a not-quite-right solution.

_____ Generate ideas about possible solutions.

_____ Restate the problem (which may or may not be the same as Step 1).

_____ Research facts, feelings, and opinions involved in the problem.

_____ Evaluate possible solutions to decide on the best ones.

_1_ State what appears to be the problem.

_____ Implement the selected decision.

_____ Evaluate the results.

_____ Recognize and reward people who contribute to resolving the problem.

_____ Look at the problem from different perspectives and other people's viewpoints.

SCORING AND INTERPRETATION

The following twelve steps to effective problem solving are listed in the order that is generally recommended by effective problem solvers.

1. State what appears to be the problem.

2. Research facts, feelings, and opinions involved in the problem.

3. Eliminate the trivial and concentrate on the major issues.

4. Restate the problem (which may or may not be the same as Step 1).

5. Look at the problem from different perspectives and other people's viewpoints.

6. Generate ideas about possible solutions.

7. Know when to stop gathering data and ideas for making a decision.

8. Evaluate possible solutions to decide on the best ones.

9. Implement the selected decision.

10. Evaluate the results.

11. Make modifications as needed in a not-quite-right solution.

12. Recognize and reward people who contribute to resolving the problem.

Congratulations if you put all the steps in the right order. You are probably known as a good problem solver and people come to you for help and ideas. You could help others by teaching them these problem-solving steps.

If you put one to four steps out of order, you can improve your problem-solving ability in the future by concentrating on following all of the steps in their correct order. You will find that it takes less time to follow the steps and solve a problem than it does to keep patching up problems with temporary solutions.

If you had more than five steps out of order, you may feel your problems never stop. You are probably feeling overwhelmed by the number of problems that need your attention. For starters, begin to use the twelve steps for problem solving above to tackle one critical problem.

QUESTIONS TO CONSIDER

1. Think of a time you successfully solved a big problem at work. What steps did you take?

2. Think of a time you struggled to solve a big problem at work. What were the biggest obstacles you faced?

3. Where did you learn your problem-solving skills? How old were you then? How do you think most people learn formally how to solve problems? Is this the best way, or is there another way that is better?

4. If someone asks you to help solve a problem, what do you usually say?

5. Why is it important to give other people recognition for their contributions to solving a problem?

Quality Improvement
How Important Is Quality?

Consumers today have high expectations for what they receive in return for spending their money on products and services. Customers are demanding, and competition for their money is increasing. Because of the increased competition, finding and retaining customers is more important than ever. Find out what you know about quality issues from the following assessment.

Instructions   The following statements are "true" (T) or "false" (F). Mark your choice on the line provided in front of each item.

_____ 1. Improved quality results in fewer customer complaints.

_____ 2. Using more employee suggestions usually results in better ways of working all around.

_____ 3. Technological advances are the secret to acquiring more customers.

_____ 4. An organization will succeed if it has the best product on the market.

_____ 5. Quality isn't tangible, so it cannot be measured.

_____ 6. The quality department is responsible for ensuring high quality; everyone else can focus on other aspects of the job.

_____ 7. The only way to succeed in business is to invent something new and sell it to a lot of customers.

_____ 8. Improving quality is every employee's job.

_____ 9. Defects and errors are inevitable, and you learn to expect a low percentage of them.

_____ 10. The only way to guarantee high quality is to have quality inspectors.

____ 11. Customers are obstacles to providing high quality because they are all different.

____ 12. Standards are set by experts in the product or service your organization provides.

____ 13. Acceptable quality is determined by customers.

____ 14. To improve quality, you must start with understanding what customers want.

SCORING AND INTERPRETATION

The following information is generally provided by quality improvement specialists and researchers. As you check your answers, think about your experiences and expectations as a customer.

1. *True.*

2. *True.*

3. *False.* Technological advances alone do not get customers. You will discover that there are other factors.

4. *False.* The best product does not guarantee buyers, so it also does not guarantee success for the company that sells the product.

5. *False.* Quality can be tangible. Think about a good apple and a bad apple. What qualities of the good apple appeal to you?

6. *False.* Today every worker is responsible for ensuring high quality.

7. *False.* There are many ways to succeed in business in addition to this one. For example, you may succeed if you resell very expensive antiques to a few customers.

8. *True.*

9. *False.* Today many organizations are changing to accept zero defects and errors.

10. *False.* There are other ways to guarantee high quality. Today quality is built into products and services all along their route to customers.

11. *False.* When customers become obstacles for any reason, the company will likely lose business. When all customers are different from one another, the company must recognize this and respond to the information.

12. *False.* Standards are set by customers.

13. *True.*

14. *True.*

If you missed no more than three items, congratulations. It appears you understand the connection between quality and customers. It probably frustrates you when people do a sloppy job and when people act as if customers are not important.

If you missed four or more items, you can learn about the connection between customer satisfaction and worker behaviors and attitudes about quality from a training session. After such a class, you will probably notice new ways you can help customers.

QUESTIONS TO CONSIDER

1. Imagine that you go to work tomorrow and there is no electricity for three hours. What can you do to maintain the quality of your work output during those three hours?

2. It has been said that workers who are unhappy spread their dissatisfaction around. How would an unhappy worker impact the quality of work on your team?

3. How does a happy worker impact the quality of work for your customers? Can you contrast the level of quality in two different places where you have worked?

4. Think of a time you were surprised and delighted to find that your newly purchased product was "worth every penny, and then some." What did you tell others about your experience? How many people did you tell? Did you act as a sales rep or a real-life advertisement for that company?

5. What do you think of the idea that responsibility for quality is everyone's job? Would you prefer to see a Quality Department or a Quality Inspection Team? What do you think most of your coworkers would prefer?

Questioning Skills
Can You Use Open-Ended and Closed Questions with Customers?

Do you know how to ask customers good questions? Appropriate and well-phrased questions at the right time can make a positive difference in customer relations. Good questions also make your job easier. Find out how well you can use open-ended or closed questions by filling out the following assessment.

Instructions   Imagine that you are a customer service representative for a small appliance manufacturing company. You have just answered a call from an angry customer who is complaining about a new, expensive toaster (a wedding gift) that does not work properly. In this phone discussion you will ask the questions listed below. Label each question according to the type of question it is.

O = Open-Ended   C = Closed

____   1. What problems are you having with your toaster?

____   2. You said this toaster was a wedding present. Is that right?

____   3. Did you say you were recently married?

____   4. What did you do the first time the toaster did that?

____   5. Can you give me an example of what you mean by that?

____   6. Are you referring to the on-off switch?

____   7. Do you have any receipts or papers with that?

____   8. Would you like me to check on that now?

____   9. What happened next?

____   10. And so you wonder if you can get another blue one?

O = Open–Ended C = Closed

____ 11. The blue one is your favorite. Is that right?

____ 12. What you want us to do is replace your toaster. Is that correct?

____ 13. Could you spell your street name for me so that I can be sure it's correct here?

____ 14. It sure makes good business sense, doesn't it?

____ 15. Is there anything else I can do for you today?

SCORING AND INTERPRETATION

The correct answers are listed below.

1. O
2. C
3. C
4. O
5. O
6. C
7. C
8. C
9. O
10. C
11. C
12. C
13. C
14. C
15. O

Did you mark all of the items correctly? Congratulations if you answered twelve to fifteen items correctly. You probably ask an appropriate mix of open-ended and closed questions to gather more information from your customers.

If you correctly answered eleven or fewer items, you will benefit from increasing your awareness of closed and open-ended questions. Many of the difficulties people experience with customers disappear when both types of questions are used appropriately.

QUESTIONS TO CONSIDER

1. Think about a time you received a satisfactory response after complaining about a defective product. How did you handle the situation when you were a customer? What happened to turn you into a satisfied customer?

2. Where did you learn how to respond to complaining customers? How old were you then? Did it seem like a natural thing to learn, or did you have to work hard at it?

3. An old saying is, "It isn't the words we hear, it's the music." What does this mean for our interactions with customers? What does this mean for customers themselves?

4. In the situation described above, the customer service representative may think the caller is attempting to take advantage of the company. What experiences have you had with a similar situation?

5. Would you treat a customer in a different way if you knew the customer was a friend or relative of your manager? Has this type of situation happened to you before?

Rewards and Recognition

How Can You Reward and Recognize Your Team Members?

It's not possible to receive too much appreciation! Your teammates are more likely to feel they are not appreciated enough. It is time to change that! Learn ways to express your appreciation from the following assessment.

Instructions   After the following numbers, list as many ways as you can think of to reward and recognize your team members. It may help to think of individual team members for inspiration, or you may think of all the ways you would like to be rewarded and recognized by others. Go for *quantity* of ideas, not quality.

1.

2.

3.

4.

5.

6.

7.

8.

9.

10.

11.

12.

13.

14.

15.

16.

17.

18.

19.

20.

SCORING AND INTERPRETATION

Instructions   If you have completed this assessment in a team situation, circle one of the items that especially appeals to you as a way to be rewarded or recognized. Put your name on your list and pass it around to your teammates, who will do the same. Read the lists you receive. On a separate sheet of paper, make notes for yourself of what types of rewards and recognition your teammates prefer. In the future you will be able to use these ideas to recognize others.

QUESTIONS TO CONSIDER

1. People are different, and different rewards appeal to different people. Have your own preferences changed during the past five years? In what way?

2. Are the costliest rewards the best rewards? Do you prefer monetary rewards? Why or why not?

3. Does public recognition embarrass you? What can you do to learn to be comfortable with receiving public recognition?

4. What are some ideas you have for recognizing your manager? Is it appropriate to recognize one's supervisor? Why or why not?

5. Managers say it is often difficult to balance the right reward with the right accomplishment. For a big project, they may want to give a big reward, but they do not want to be perceived as playing favorites. What ideas do you have about how to overcome this perception? How can managers best be equitable in rewarding employees?

Risk Taking
Are You a Risk Taker at Work?

Every job has risks. Do you automatically take risks, or do you tend to play it safe? People differ in their willingness to take risks, and people are willing to take different kinds of risks. Some take personal, work-related, physical, or financial risks. For others, security is the most important thing, so they stay away from taking any type of risk.

Instructions   Read each statement below and rate yourself according to the following scale.

1 = Not like me   2 = Sometimes/often like me   3 = Usually like me

____   1. I work best in an orderly and predictable environment.

____   2. I prefer to do things in ways that have already been proven.

____   3. I prefer to work with established routines.

____   4. I like to wait until I have all the facts before making a decision.

____   5. I am uncomfortable with new procedures that are not yet proven.

____   6. I will stay in a bad situation rather than make an uncertain change.

____   7. I prefer to make changes slowly and in small steps.

____   8. I usually don't tell anyone if I do think of a good idea about a change to make.

____   9. I worry that I will say or do the wrong thing in front of my boss.

____ 10. I worry about the impression I make on other people.

____ 11. I become anxious about doing something new.

____ 12. I like experimenting with new ways to do my work.

____ 13. I enjoy bringing up new ideas at meetings.

____ 14. I feel comfortable and confident taking on a new project.

____ 15. I enjoy acting on a hunch to see what will happen.

1 = Not like me   2 = Sometimes/often like me   3 = Usually like me

____ 16. I like to go to new places for no other reason than to see what's there.

____ 17. I want to experience as much of life as possible.

____ 18. I have a strong need for excitement and variety in my life.

____ 19. I like to change things around just for the sake of making changes.

____ 20. I have fun on the scary rides at amusement parks.

____ 21. My closest friends are risk takers.

SCORING AND INTERPRETATION

Instructions   First total your responses for items 1 through 11 and put your total here: _____

Next total your responses for items 12 through 21 and put your total here: _____

If your total score for items 1 through 11 is 15 or lower and your total score for items 12 through 21 is 25 or higher, you like challenges and prefer variety instead of a routine work environment. Adventures charge your batteries, so you seek variety and excitement. Your job satisfaction comes from being able to take risks.

If your total score for items 1 through 11 is 25 or higher and your total score for items 12 through 21 is 15 or lower, you like a routine and predictable work life. You prefer to let others experiment with new ways of doing things as you stay away from new and different ways. One of your goals is to maintain a secure and well-ordered work life.

If your scores do not fit either of these patterns, your choices indicate that you enjoy some risk taking and you are open to some new experiences that could be called risky. However, you are security conscious and like quite a bit of routine and predictability in your work life. Some people in this group are risk takers in their personal lives and they are not risk takers in their work lives, or vice versa.

QUESTIONS TO CONSIDER

1. Some risks are easier to take than others. Describe a big risk taken by someone you know.

2. Has anything happened in your life that changed you from being a risk taker to not being as willing to take risks? Or has anything happened that changed you into a risk taker?

3. What is "job security" in today's work world? What would it take for a person to have job security for the future?

4. Researchers advise taking tiny risks, one at a time, to build up risk-taking skills. What tiny risks could you take in your present work environment?

5. What does the statement, "Give yourself permission to overestimate yourself" mean for a person who is not a risk taker? Could it have any meaning for your own life?

Stress Management

Do You Know How to Manage Personal Stress?

Stress is your body's response to new or difficult situations. It is important to build up your resistance to stress. There are several ways to do this. How well are you doing? Find out by filling out the following assessment.

Instructions For each of the statements below, rate yourself on the following scale.

5 = Always   3 = Usually   1 = Seldom

____ 1. I manage my time effectively.

____ 2. I use assertive statements to protect my right to say "no" to others.

____ 3. I regularly share my feelings with someone close to me.

____ 4. I do community volunteer work that is meaningful to me.

____ 5. I eat a balanced diet with lots of fresh fruits and vegetables.

____ 6. I do aerobic exercise at least three times each week.

____ 7. I practice relaxation techniques daily.

____ 8. I avoid unhealthy habits for coping with stress.

____ 9. I spend some leisure time in a place where I have a complete change of scenery.

____ 10. I have talked with my boss about my work commitments and expectations.

____ 11. I have talked with members of my household to divide up responsibilities.

____ 12. I get enough sleep every night.

Total: _____

SCORING AND INTERPRETATION

Instructions   Total your score and write it on the line above. A score of 50 to 60 indicates that you are doing the right things to manage your stress level. Have an annual medical checkup and keep doing the right things.

If your score is between 36 and 49, you are taking many steps to manage your stress successfully, but there is more you can do. It may be a challenge to add more into your day, so rethink your priorities. Ask friends and family to help you.

If your score is 35 or lower, you are pointing yourself in the direction of health problems and wrecked relationships at work and at home. Run, do not walk, to the next stress management class you can take. Make an appointment for a physical checkup and talk with your health care provider about your stress concerns.

QUESTIONS TO CONSIDER

1. "In the old days people didn't have the same type of stress as they have these days." What are your ideas about this statement?

2. Improving your communication skills can help reduce your stress level. Can you describe ways in which good communication skills help with stress management?

Assessments A to Z/© 2000 Jossey-Bass/Pfeiffer

3. "Friends are good medicine." Explain this concept to someone close to you. What will you say?

4. Changing what you eat and the ways in which you eat may be the most difficult changes you ever take on. Why is this so?

5. Do you expect to experience more or less stress in the next ten years? What plans can you make to deal with upcoming stress?

Team Decision Making

What Are the Benefits of Team Decision Making?

Team decision making may take longer than individual decision making, but in most situations the advantages outweigh the disadvantages. Learn the benefits by taking the following assessment.

Instructions   The following list of benefits of team decision making contains one false statement. Circle the false statement.

1. Individual viewpoints are expressed during team decision making.

2. More opinions and ideas are offered for consideration.

3. Members obtain new ideas to piggyback on ideas of others.

4. People's self-interest surfaces so decisions can incorporate them.

5. Personal learning and growth occur from being around others.

6. Skills in decision making are increased.

7. More thought and energy are devoted to important decisions.

8. Group members are influenced by others to commit to the decision; they are not forced.

9. Members who are quiet are expected to contribute their ideas.

10. The member who suggested the idea that is chosen gets to decide how it will be implemented.

11. Members become committed to the team decision.

12. There is stronger unity among team members.

SCORING AND INTERPRETATION

Only number 10 above is false. All of the other statements are true benefits of team decision making. Effective teams do not keep track of who "owns" the ideas for the best decision. In fact, in effective teams the members contribute so much to an original idea that it is soon unrecognizable to the person who offered it.

QUESTIONS TO CONSIDER

1. Describe a positive experience you have had with team decision making.

2. Think about your first experience on a team at work. Did you like the experience right away or did you feel uncomfortable? What do you suppose most people experience?

3. What are two good ways to persuade quiet team members to contribute their ideas to a decision-making discussion?

4. What is an effective way to urge an overly talkative team member to allow others to talk? Could anyone on the team handle this type of situation, or should only certain members step in?

5. What ideas do you have for confronting team members who leave a team meeting and tell others that the great ideas they had were shot down by the team?

ℐeamwork
What Are Your Responsibilities as a Team Member?

Team members have different personalities and different ways of accomplishing work. When working together on a team, all members are called on to use their best interpersonal skills. Discover what you know about your responsibilities as a team member by taking the following assessment.

Instructions   Think about a team you are on now and write on the blank in front of each item whether you agree (A) or disagree (D) with the statement. Choose the best answer for your own behavior.

_____   1. I spend social time with team members to get to know them better.

_____   2. I urge team members to communicate clearly and honestly.

_____   3. I encourage everyone to discuss any issues they may have with the entire team.

_____   4. I bring my best skills and attitude to my team.

_____   5. I expect only the best from members of my team, and they know it.

_____   6. I help turn team problems into opportunities.

_____   7. I value the differences of viewpoint and varied experiences on our team.

_____   8. I back up my team members when they need help.

_____   9. I share what I learn with team members.

_____   10. I bring good news as well as bad news to team meetings.

_____   11. I remind team members how important it is to maintain trust among members of the team.

_____   12. I assume a leadership role when it is appropriate for me to do so.

SCORING AND INTERPRETATION

If you responded to each item with an A for "agree," you are doing your part to create good team member relationships and communication.

If you did not agree with from one to three items, look back at those items. Were you questioning your skills and abilities as you answered? Did you have a specific, challenging situation in mind? Is this indicative of an unusual situation? Are you working to improve this situation?

If you disagreed with four or more statements, you may be surprised to learn that team members question your participation on this team. It appears you avoid making contributions to the team. Can you determine what reasons you may have for this behavior. Do team members understand why you participate so little? What can you do to improve this situation?

QUESTIONS TO CONSIDER

1. Most organizations have people work in teams. What are three reasons for doing this?

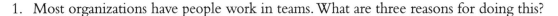

2. Teams hold meetings to do their work. What ideas do you have to make team meetings more productive? What is one action step you can take to help improve your next team meeting?

Assessments A to Z/© 2000 Jossey-Bass/Pfeiffer

3. What have been some of your experiences with a highly productive team? What made the experiences so successful?

4. Do you think that teams are here to stay, or are they a passing fad? Why do you think that?

5. Teams typically go through a beginning stage during which members get to know one another. What are the benefits of getting to know other team members both professionally and personally? What happens when a team omits "getting to know you" activities?

Telecommuting
What Questions Do You Have About Telecommuting?

Managers are often unprepared to supervise workers who are based at home, so they may avoid letting employees telecommute for as long as possible. However, increasing numbers of people are working at home successfully, and it has been found that there are major advantages for the organization, for society, and for individuals who work from home. Check out the questions you have about telecommuting by taking the following assessment.

Instructions   On the line in front of each statement, make a check mark if this is a question you have about telecommuting.

_____ 1. How will I know whether telecommuters are really working?

_____ 2. If they are at home, how will they obtain the information they need for their work?

_____ 3. Do telecommuters work fewer hours than office-based workers?

_____ 4. What different management skills are needed to manage telecommuters?

_____ 5. Could my entire staff telecommute?

_____ 6. Will all my staff want to telecommute?

_____ 7. Am I required to make home visits or home office checkups?

_____ 8. Who purchases the computer and other electronic equipment that a telecommuter needs?

_____ 9. How can I tell what equipment is actually needed?

_____ 10. Who purchases the office furniture? What furniture does a home worker need?

_____ 11. How would I handle office supply purchases?

_____ 12. How can the company be sure that its data is secure?

____ 13. Are we required to purchase some kind of extra insurance for people who work at home?

____ 14. What safety issues are my responsibility?

____ 15. How do telecommuters stay in contact with people in the office?

____ 16. What happens if a telecommuter is injured at home while working?

____ 17. Will we hear baby and dog noises when we call telecommuters on business?

____ 18. What if I need a telecommuter at the office when the person is at home?

____ 19. How can I arrange for telecommuters to attend meetings?

____ 20. Will those who are not allowed to telecommute be resentful?

SCORING AND INTERPRETATION

If you have checked seventeen to twenty items, you are not unusual. Most managers who are new to the management of telecommuters have many questions. Specific training on these issues will help you understand the process and help you avoid problems. If you checked only a few questions, you probably have some experience with managing telecommuters or telecommuting yourself. This means you can help other managers with their concerns during a training session.

QUESTIONS TO CONSIDER

1. What are some of the major advantages for an organization that has telecommuters?

2. Most people struggle with new ways of working and workplace changes. What can managers do to ease into a telecommuting program?

3. "Managing is managing." What does this statement mean to you in relation to telecommuting?

4. How important is establishing a trusting relationship with an employee in a telecommuting situation? What can be done to increase trust between a manager and a telecommuter?

5. What experiences have you had with new programs that were successful immediately? Can you use some of the ideas that worked well for you then to help you create a successful telecommuting program?

Time Management
Can You Sequence Ten Steps for Effective Time Management?

Effective time management reduces stress and increases your efficiency at work. When you are assigned a new project, taking certain time-management steps in a proper sequence will help you budget your time to complete the project. Learn how to do this from the following assessment.

Instructions   Assume you have been given a new project to complete. What will you do first? Second? Third? Put the following list of ten time-management steps in the proper sequence to obtain the most effective results. Write the correct number on the line next to each item, that is, label the first step "1," the second step "2," and so on.

____   Make decisions about the proper sequence of your tasks.

____   Schedule your most important tasks.

____   Avoid scheduling every minute of your day.

____   Break your project into small pieces or tasks.

____   List your tasks.

____   Cross off tasks as they are completed.

____   Schedule your remaining tasks.

____   Stick to your schedule.

____   Prioritize your tasks.

____   List important tasks to do the following day.

SCORING AND INTERPRETATION

According to most time management experts, you will obtain the best results from the following sequence:

1. Break your project into small pieces or tasks.

2. List your tasks.

3. Prioritize your tasks.

4. Make decisions about the proper sequence of your tasks.

5. Schedule your most important tasks.

6. Schedule your remaining tasks.

7. Avoid scheduling every minute of your day.

8. Stick to your schedule.

9. Cross tasks off as they are completed.

10. List important tasks to do the following day.

If your list matches exactly, congratulations. You know how to manage your time effectively to accomplish your work. Perhaps you could offer suggestions to help others who are unsure of the best ways to manage their time.

If you had more than two items in a different order, challenge yourself to experiment with three new time-management techniques during the next week. You will be pleased with the results.

QUESTIONS TO CONSIDER

1. How did you learn how to manage your time? Do you remember who taught you? How old were you when you started managing your time?

2. Do you feel you have less time to accomplish your projects at work these days? Do you believe your coworkers also have increased time pressures?

3. What happened in the past when you did less important tasks before the most important tasks of a project?

4. "Even your priorities have priorities." What does this statement mean to you?

5. Some people miss deadlines and forget important meetings because of poor time management. What generally happens to morale around the workplace when these things happen?

Training Design
Do You Know the Steps to Training Design?

Training programs do not happen by spontaneous combustion. They are the result of many steps that are taken in a certain sequence by the program designer. Do you know the proper sequence? Check your knowledge by taking the following assessment.

Instructions   Read each of the following eight steps to designing a training program. They are not in the proper sequence. Put them in order by writing the appropriate number on the line prior to each item.

_____ Set general learning goals.

_____ Revise design details.

_____ Start detailed planning.

_____ Specify objectives.

_____ Sequence training activities.

_____ Design training activities.

_____ Assess participants.

_____ Evaluate the total results.

SCORING AND INTERPRETATION

Following is the sequence of steps recommended by effective training designers.

1. Assess participants.

2. Set general learning goals.

3. Specify objectives.

4. Design training activities.

5. Sequence training activities.

6. Start detailed planning.

7. Revise design details.

8. Evaluate the total results.

Did you put the steps in their proper order? If you switched two steps, look back to see how this would impact the results of a training program. Most likely it would make a big difference. If you had more than two of the steps out of order, you can learn more about design by taking a training-design course. You will immediately notice the increased effectiveness of your training designs if you begin using the steps in their proper order.

QUESTIONS TO CONSIDER

1. What experiences have you had when you took training programs that were well-designed? How did you know they were well-designed programs?

2. What is involved with the assessment of participants in the first step? Why is this step so important?

3. Some people think it takes too long to go through all eight steps. What are your ideas about this?

4. Most trainers who design programs have a favorite and least favorite design step. What is your favorite step? What is your least favorite step? Explain why in each case.

5. "One of the best ways to improve your training design skills is to go to the training programs of people with excellent reputations and learn from them." What are your thoughts about this statement?

Training Techniques

Which Training Techniques Do You Practice?

"You just go to the front of the room and start telling the group what you know. That's training." No, that's not all there is to training. Adult educators have discovered that telling isn't teaching, and much has been written and published about effective methods and techniques to help learners. See how many you are familiar with by taking the following assessment.

Instructions How often do you use the following training techniques? For each of the following statements, rate yourself on the scale below and place the appropriate number in the space provided.

1 = Never   2 = Sometimes   3 = Always

____ 1. I make learning agreements with participants at the beginning of a training session.

____ 2. I ask questions that I have prepared in advance.

____ 3. I use participants' names as much as possible.

____ 4. I ask questions to clarify something when I see confused expressions.

____ 5. I ask everyone to move around and sit with other participants.

____ 6. I ask participants whether they have questions, comments, or suggestions.

____ 7. I use games.

____ 8. I use role plays.

____ 9. I add writing exercises into the mix.

1 = Never   2 = Sometimes   3 = Always

____ 10. I use visual aids.

____ 11. I use appropriate humor.

____ 12. I balance quiet times with active times.

____ 13. I ask participants to prepare and deliver parts of the training.

____ 14. I ask participants to do demonstrations of their learning.

Total: _____

SCORING AND INTERPRETATION

Instructions Add your responses and put the total on the line following the statements.

If your total is between 35 and 42, you are doing an excellent job using a variety of effective training techniques. You probably have your favorites, and you may want to challenge yourself to expand your repertoire of techniques.

If your total is between 28 and 34, you are using some effective training methods and you can increase the list of possibilities. You may want to talk with other trainers and ask them for their most effective training methods.

If your total is below 28, you will benefit greatly from learning new training methods. In addition, by expanding your repertoire you will have more satisfied trainees who learn more of what you are teaching them.

QUESTIONS TO CONSIDER

1. Where did you learn your training skills? What words would you use to describe your experiences as a trainer, starting from your first training experience?

2. Have you seen effective trainers in action? What especially effective methods have you seen them use? Could you adopt these methods for yourself?

3. Do young people say, "I want to grow up to be a trainer"? How do people get into training work?

4. Have you ever been a hostage in a training program or class? What did you do about it? How did it impact your learning?

5. "Some trainers are better than others." How would you describe what "better" means in that statement?

Assessments A to Z/© 2000 Jossey-Bass/Pfeiffer

Upset Customers
Do You Know Proven Ways to Calm Upset Customers?

Anyone who has customers must learn to calm them when they are upset before providing continued service. Calming upset customers is difficult to do, but by taking the following assessment you can learn what you already know about the topic and learn some new things.

Instructions   Read each statement below and rate yourself on the following scale on how well you practice each of the techniques. Give yourself a 1 if you already do this well more than 95 percent of the time. Rate yourself a 2 if you need improvement on this aspect of customer service.

1 = Do well   2 = Need improvement

____ 1. I give customers an opportunity to explain why they are upset.

____ 2. I listen for details while upset customers tell their stories.

____ 3. I look at the problem from the customer's point of view.

____ 4. I tell upset customers I'm sorry they are having problems.

____ 5. I avoid blaming anyone for what is wrong.

____ 6. I do not take it personally when upset customers blame me.

____ 7. I look for ways to correct problems that customers have.

____ 8. I ask upset customers what solutions they want.

____ 9. I make a written list of what an upset customer wants.

____ 10. I carefully select my words to avoid arguments with upset customers.

____ 11. I tell upset customers when we cannot provide their preferred solutions, and I explain the reasons to them.

1 = Do well   2 = Need improvement

____ 12. I offer alternative solutions when possible.

____ 13. I ask upset customers about their reactions to my possible solutions.

____ 14. I finish with upset customers by asking whether they would agree that we took care of their problems.

____ 15. I thank customers for doing business with us.

____ 16. I check back with upset customers to make sure their problems were resolved to their satisfaction.

Total: _____

SCORING AND INTERPRETATION

Instructions Total your responses and put the number on the line following the statements. The closer your total is to 16, the better you are at dealing with upset customers.

If your score is over 22, you will benefit from some training to increase your customer relations skills. This will reduce your stress level at work, too. There are many ways you can improve your contacts with upset customers, including training and self-help books and videos.

If your score is between 28 and 32, you can greatly reduce your stress level and increase your success level with customers by learning and applying new techniques.

QUESTIONS TO CONSIDER

1. Some people take great pride in being able to win over the grouchiest and angriest customers. How valuable are these people to their employers?

2. "How can you *not* take it personally when someone is yelling at you and calling you names?" asks a very frustrated new employee. How would you respond to this question?

3. If it is true that people learn from their mistakes, what mistakes have you made that now help you calm upset customers? In what ways could you help a new employee to benefit from your experiences?

4. When you are having a bad week because of a situation at home, what are some ways to keep your home life and your work life separated? Assuming you are already irritable, in what ways could you make sure you have patience and good listening skills with upset customers?

5. "Because it's against company policy." How do you react to this statement? Would this statement help you to calm an upset customer so you could respond to his or her complaint? Why or why not?

     Assessments A to Z/© 2000 Jossey-Bass/Pfeiffer

Values
What Are Your Most Important Work Values?

Work values are ideas and attitudes that are so personally important that people structure their lives around them. For most people, work values change somewhat during their careers. Work values are not to be seen as "right" or "wrong," but they are different for different people. Check yours by taking the following assessment.

Instructions   Read the following list of work values and determine the five that are the most important to you at this time in your life and that you feel you must obtain from your job. Underline those five values.

Acceptance	Equality	Knowledge	Security
Achievement	Family	Loyalty	Self-Esteem
Advancement	Friendship	Money	Self-Respect
Challenge	Health	Peace	Spirituality
Competence	Honesty	Pleasure	Success
Creativity	Independence	Possessions	Wisdom
Dignity	Integrity	Power	

SCORING AND INTERPRETATION

Instructions   Write the five work values you selected in the right-hand column below.

_____   _____

_____   _____

_____   _____

_____   _____

_____   _____

Now rank the values you selected by numbering them from 1 (most important) to 5 (least important) in the left-hand column.

It is difficult for some people to prioritize their top work values. For others it is easier to do. Look at what you indicated above as your top values. It may help you manage your work life better if you consider these values on a regular basis and compare them with what is going on in your workplace.

People's work values often shift in priority; as their lives change, their priorities change. If your job takes too much of your energy, or you want to do some other kind of work, consider your values before changing positions. Your values are the key to help you make the right changes in your work life. You invite conflict and unhappiness if you do not honor your personal work values. Some people do a career checkup at the end of a year, on their birthdays, or at another scheduled time. It's a good way to stay effective and satisfied on the job.

QUESTIONS TO CONSIDER

1. Some people might say, "You are lucky to have a job, so never mind whether your job makes you happy." What do you think of this statement?

2. Can you recall a time at work when your personal values conflicted with what your employer expected you to do? How did you feel about that at the time? What did you do about the situation?

3. Are there any important work values you would add to the list above?

4. Think about your first job. What were your most important work values at that time? How are they different from the ones you hold today? How are they the same as your values today?

5. When you selected your top values from the list above, was it difficult to select only five? Did you find ways to combine some of the values? Did you select one or two top values and consider the remaining values of lesser importance? Explain the process you used and why it worked for you.

Visual Aids

Do You Use Visual Aids Effectively?

By using visual aids in your training programs, you help trainees learn more effectively. Information is then presented through two channels at once: eyes and ears. Whether you use visual aids prepared in advance or create your visual aids as you go, there are certain ways to use them most effectively. Learn how well you use visual aids by taking the following assessment.

Instructions All of the following tips for using visual aids are true except two items. Identify the two that are *not* true and circle them in the following list.

1. Show a visual aid while you are talking about it.

2. You may want to introduce a visual aid before showing it so that people are somewhat prepared for the message they are about to see.

3. Take enough time to allow the audience to see and understand your visual aid.

4. When you are not talking about a visual aid, conceal it from the audience so they can concentrate on what they are hearing.

5. Explain visual aids adequately, because not everyone in the audience has the same background and understanding you have.

6. Use color when possible, and make sure your information is readable when you show it to your audience.

7. When you have handout materials, you can use the handout for a visual aid even when it consists of a full page of text.

8. Be sure people in the back of the room can see the visual aids.

9. Be sure your body does not block anyone's view of the visual aid.

10. Limit the amount of information on a visual to a single main idea.

11. Talk to your audience, not to your visual or to the equipment.

12. Point with your arm that is nearest the screen so that your body faces the audience at all times.

13. The more visual aids you use the better. Use visual aids to illustrate every point you make in your program.

14. Test all of the equipment in advance.

15. Check to make sure that your visual aids are in proper sequence.

16. Anticipate potential equipment problems and arrange solutions in advance.

SCORING AND INTERPRETATION

The only items that are false are numbers 7 and 13. If you circled only these items, congratulations. You have excellent command of using visual aids when presenting to an audience. You know the best way to present visuals and that handout material is for all additional information. You could be a good mentor for someone who is beginning to use visual aids for presentations.

If you missed one to three items, you make a few mistakes when presenting with visual aids, and your skills will improve now that you know the correct methods. Next time you present with visual aids, you will be pleased to discover you are no longer making these mistakes.

If you missed four or more items, you will benefit from learning new methods of presenting with visual aids. In addition, you may want to ask someone who already presents well to mentor you for a few presentations.

QUESTIONS TO CONSIDER

1. Think of a time you attended a fascinating presentation. What visual aids did the presenter use? How were they used by the presenter? Which of those methods and techniques could you copy?

2. A small percentage of people are unable to see reds and greens the way most people do. What does this suggest for using color with your visuals? What other ideas do you have about using color for visual aids?

3. What is your opinion about using visual aids for a short presentation, say fifteen to twenty-five minutes? How would you spread visual aids over an all-day presentation? What ideas do you have for using visual aids after a meal break? During a meal? When do you think are the best and worst times to use visual aids?

4. Today's technology enables presenters to use a lot of sizzle and razzle-dazzle. To what extent will you be using all the fancy features and equipment available today? What presentation methods would you like to use if money were no object?

5. If you had fifty points to divide between "sizzle" and "substance" for a work presentation, how will you divide your points? Why?

Voice Control

Are You Able to Modulate Your Voice Over the Telephone?

How you sound gives people a positive or a negative impression of you. Your voice is a delicate instrument, and you can learn to play it. Do you know how to make your voice work for you when making important telephone calls? Check your knowledge by taking the following assessment.

Instructions   Each statement below has one *best* answer. Circle the letter of the best answer.

1. When you make a phone call in a wide-open area
   a. speak in your normal conversational tone
   b. lower your voice and pitch
   c. speak louder than you usually would

2. When you have a bad phone connection
   a. speak louder than you usually would
   b. raise your pitch two levels
   c. insist on calling back

3. When you make a stressful phone call
   a. speak in your usual voice
   b. speak louder than usual
   c. lower your speaking voice

4. Before you make an important phone call
   a. rehearse your opening words
   b. do not rehearse, so you will be spontaneous
   c. eat something sweet

5. When you begin a business phone conversation

    a. keep the pitch of your voice just above your regular tone

    b. keep the pitch of your voice just below your regular tone

    c. talk fast and say as much as possible at the beginning

6. If you have a regional or foreign accent

    a. immediately tell people where you are from

    b. study and eliminate your accent

    c. forget about it unless people have trouble understanding you

7. Speak in short sentences using everyday words and you will sound

    a. unsure of yourself

    b. confident and sure of yourself

    c. like a trainee

8. When you expect questions and have answers in advance

    a. you sound rehearsed and phony when answering questions

    b. you can make notes while you are answering questions

    c. you are smart and you will sound confident when answering questions

9. If you are reading a script

    a. practice it aloud until you are comfortable saying the entire thing

    b. add in whatever you think improves the script

    c. speak as quickly as possible so it sounds natural

10. To emphasize an important point

    a. pause after saying the important thought

    b. pause before saying the important thought

    c. speak louder than usual while saying it

11. Callers do not see you while you are talking on the telephone with them, so you

    a. can slouch in your chair if you want to

    b. can catch up on your paperwork while they talk

    c. need to smile and put friendliness in your voice

12. The best reason to look into a mirror during a telephone conversation is

    a. to see whether you have food stuck in your teeth

    b. to watch yourself getting older every day at work

    c. to remind you to smile

SCORING AND INTERPRETATION

Instructions   The correct answers are given below. Circle any items you answered incorrectly.

1. b
2. c
3. a
4. a
5. a
6. c
7. b
8. c
9. a
10. a
11. c
12. c

If you missed zero to two items, congratulations. You are aware of your voice and how to use it effectively on the telephone. You could be a mentor for someone who is developing new telephone skills.

If you missed three to six items, you know some ways to use your voice most effectively on the telephone. You will learn additional ways. Your confidence will increase and you will be happy with the results.

If you missed more than six items, you have many new things to learn about using your voice effectively on the telephone. The results of using your new skills will please you. Some people never give a thought to managing their voices. However, just as most famous singers use voice coaches to help them improve their skills, you can improve your voice skills with coaching.

QUESTIONS TO CONSIDER

1. What training were you given for speaking on the telephone at your first job?

2. Have you ever been impressed by the sound of someone's voice on the telephone? What did you like about it? What would it take for you to sound more like this person?

3. Actors and singers learn breathing techniques in their voice classes. How could you benefit from learning more about proper breathing for voice control? How could you arrange to talk to someone who knows about this?

4. Have you ever received a call from someone who was reading a script to you? How soon did you know there was a script? How did you feel about this caller? How did you respond to this call?

5. There is an old saying that says, "If you end up with the lemons, use them to make lemonade." How does this saying relate to a person who has an accent? How can people know when to learn new ways of speaking and when to leave their unique ways of speaking alone?

Work Life
Does Your Job Make You Unhappy?

Many people tell career counselors that they hate their jobs. But often they don't really hate their jobs; they are only unhappy with some aspect of their work conditions. Every workplace is different, and these differences can affect morale and job performance—and even spill over to employees' home lives. See how happy you are in your current job by filling out the following assessment.

Instructions   Read the following statements, think about your current job, and mark whether you "agree" (A) or "disagree" (D) with each statement.

A = Agree   D = Disagree

_____   1.   The work I do is interesting and I enjoy it.

_____   2.   I like my coworkers.

_____   3.   I have a great boss.

_____   4.   The pay here is acceptable for now.

_____   5.   I like the benefits that come with this job.

_____   6.   People here are conscientious about their work.

_____   7.   People here work efficiently.

_____   8.   People here seem to like working here.

_____   9.   People here work together to get work done.

_____ 10.   The pace here is good for me.

_____ 11.   There is a good mix of "try new things" and "stick with tried-and-true."

_____ 12.   My work load does not overwhelm me.

A = Agree   D = Disagree

____ 13. I have the right amount of personal freedom here.

____ 14. The lighting in my work area suits me.

____ 15. The air temperature here suits me.

____ 16. The air quality here suits me.

____ 17. I believe I work in a safe work environment.

____ 18. The size of my work area suits me.

____ 19. The noise level in my work area is not a problem.

____ 20. My work schedule is the one I want.

____ 21. Rules and regulations here make sense, and I have no problems with them.

____ 22. I know what it takes to get a raise in pay when I want more money.

____ 23. Work assignments here are matched to the right people.

____ 24. Management takes an interest in workers here.

Total A Responses: _____

SCORING AND INTERPRETATION

Instructions Total the number of your A (agree) responses and put the number on the line above.

If this number is 20 or higher, you appear to have a good match with your work situation and your preferences. Most people would say you seem very happy with your job.

If your total number of A responses is between 15 and 19, there are many aspects of your current job that are a good match, and many aspects that are a poor match. Look back at your responses and select one of the problem areas you identified with a D (disagree) response. Are there ways you could improve this situation? Ask others for their advice.

If your total number is below 15, you are like the people who tell career counselors they hate their jobs. You may want to give serious thought to making an appointment with a career counselor to help you determine a new career direction and plan job search activities.

QUESTIONS TO CONSIDER

1. How happy do you think people deserve to be at work?

2. Is work a place to go or a thing to do? What is the meaning of work in your life?

3. If you have a bad match with your job, and it comes down to (a) accept it, (b) change it, or (c) move on, what seems to be the best option for you?

4. Some people are willing to put up with working conditions that other people will not tolerate for a week. What are your thoughts on this?

5. When you were a child, what did you hear adults saying about work and work conditions? In what ways have you been influenced by what you heard then?

Workaholism
Are You Working Too Much?

Workaholism has been called the disastrous disease everyone applauds. When you were a child complaining about doing your chores, an adult may have told you, "Nobody ever died from overwork." Today, it happens. People who devote their lives to their work often develop serious health problems, and some people die from them. Is this where you want your career to take you? To check your attitude and work habits to find out whether you are in a danger zone, take the following assessment.

Instructions For each of the following statements, consider your attitude and your behavior and, on the line provided, mark the response that most nearly describes the real you according to the scale below.

1 = Definitely not true   2 = Usually true   3 = Mostly true   4 = Definitely true

____ 1. I am working most of the time when I am not sleeping.

____ 2. I enjoy my work, so for now I don't have interests in other things.

____ 3. My time with friends and family is very limited—maybe a few hours each year.

____ 4. I want to have a special relationship with someone, but I am too busy now.

____ 5. I am too busy at work to have a regular exercise and fitness program.

____ 6. I do not have time for a hobby. My work is my hobby.

____ 7. "Why would I sit around and do nothing?" you honestly ask yourself.

____ 8. I am too busy to get an annual physical exam.

____ 9. Well-meaning people advise me to slow down, take some time off, and relax.

____ 10. People don't understand that my fun is my work.

Total: _____

SCORING AND INTERPRETATION

Instructions Total your responses and put your total on the line above.

A score over 30 indicates that very strong workaholic attitudes and habits are running your life right now. Undoubtedly, you believe this is more positive than negative news. However, research warns us that the opposite is true, and you are jeopardizing your health and well-being. If you answered the above questions with someone who does not have workaholic tendencies and habits, you would realize the differences between your world views. It is likely that the closer your score is to 40, the more denial you have about the consequences of your workaholic behavior. Consider the results of this assessment as a warning and find ways to begin making changes in your behavior.

A score between 20 and 30 indicates a potential problem with workaholism. It is time to reevaluate your attitudes and behavior and change your workaholic ways. Look back over your responses and find those marked 3 and 4. These point to your most troublesome areas. Select one item to experiment with during the next month. For example, you may want to sit around and do nothing for three hours if number 7 is the item you select. Ask someone you trust to help you with this.

A score below 20 indicates you are successfully avoiding workaholic attitudes and behaviors. The lower your score, the better. Look back at any responses you marked with a 2 or higher. These indicate potential trouble spots, and you may want to take steps now to prevent problems in the future. Congratulations for having a healthy attitude about the place of work in your life.

QUESTIONS TO CONSIDER

1. Where do people get their ideas about how much work is "too much" or "not enough"? Did you have a role model in mind as you answered the questions? What or who has influenced your work attitudes and behaviors?

2. Researchers have called workaholism a disease. They have compared workaholism to alcoholism because of the addictiveness involved in each, the chemical changes that take place in the body, and the lifestyle that characterizes these diseases. Were you aware of this? In what ways does this similarity apply to you? Where could you find someone to give you a trusted, objective opinion of your situation?

3. Think back to your childhood and teen years. Did you have workaholic tendencies and attitudes then? In what ways did adults around you work? Were you personally impacted because of the work habits of someone in your family?

4. Assume for a moment that your best friend or dearest relative has an addiction of some sort. It's obvious to you that this person will die if something doesn't change. You have talked to this person before. Others have talked to this person. Things are only worse. How would you feel about this? Can you find similarities between this person's situation and your own situation if you are a workaholic?

5. If you were guaranteed to find fame, fortune, and happiness for *failing* at something, what would you do? How soon would you start?

            Assessments A to Z/© 2000 Jossey-Bass/Pfeiffer

X-Tra for Trainers

Are You an Effective Trainer?

Trainers influence the attitudes and skills of others. Working with individuals or groups of any size, trainers enable people to learn something new that will increase their effectiveness at work. Check the effectiveness of your training skills by taking the following assessment.

Instructions   Read each statement and rate yourself according to the following scale.

1 = Never   2 = Rarely   3 = Sometimes   4 = Usually   5 = Always

____ 1. I assess the training needs of each group prior to the start of training and use the information to develop appropriate content.

____ 2. To prepare for a class I review the selected materials, activities, and the sequence of events at least two days in advance.

____ 3. I greet trainees as they are entering the training area.

____ 4. After a training group assembles, I ask trainees what they know about the topic before I begin teaching the material.

____ 5. I ask trainees to remove sources of distractions and interruptions (pagers, cell phones, and novels) to better concentrate on the training material.

____ 6. I make the objectives of a class available to participants in both written and verbal forms.

____ 7. I ask for feedback from trainees several times during a training session.

____ 8. I look for ways to energize my teaching style with activities, stories, visual aids, and so forth.

____ 9. I make it a point to be a good example for trainees by starting, stopping, and returning from breaks on time.

1 = Never   2 = Rarely   3 = Sometimes   4 = Usually   5 = Always

____ 10. I use flip charts, overhead projectors, and computer technology to help deliver training materials.

____ 11. I make print and other visual material colorful and interesting when possible.

____ 12. I vary learning methods by using lecture, structured discussions, case studies, role plays, games, and so forth.

____ 13. I monitor my nonverbal delivery skills, such as my posture and facial expressions, that could be misinterpreted as boredom or disapproval.

____ 14. I ask trainees for examples of how the training material can be used on their jobs.

____ 15. I use a special technique that is fun and effective to bring trainees back from breaks on time.

____ 16. I read publications, take classes, and visit Websites to learn ways to improve my training.

____ 17. When trainees appear confused about something, I ask them whether I can help clarify.

____ 18. I vary my teaching for visual, oral, and tactile learners because everyone learns in different ways.

____ 19. I use good meeting management skills.

____ 20. I use good group management and group process skills.

____ 21. To gauge the effectiveness of my training, I follow up with surveys, e-mail, or phone calls.

____ 22. I am learning to use new technology for increasing my teaching effectiveness.

Total: _____

SCORING AND INTERPRETATION

Instructions   Write your total score on the line above. If your score is 98 to 110, you are doing what the most effective trainers do so they can positively influence the attitudes and skills of their participants. In addition you are probably developing new ways to increase your effectiveness in the learning sessions you lead.

If your score is 83 to 97, you are usually an effective trainer and you can increase your effectiveness. Look at your responses that are not 5's. These indicate areas in which to seek improvements that will increase your effectiveness.

If your score is below 83, your training skills can be greatly improved, and both you and your training participants will benefit. There are several situations in which you may be an expert in the material you are presenting, but your methods call for modification. Particularly notice any items you answered with a 3 or less. These are your weakest areas and the areas to focus on for skill building.

QUESTIONS TO CONSIDER

1. What do you recall about the style, methods, or the program of the most effective trainer you have ever seen working? What do you recall about the least effective trainer you have ever seen working? What is one thing the most effective trainer prompted you to do?

2. In what ways do the general attitudes of trainers influence trainees? What are your ideas about the contagiousness of energy and enthusiasm during a training session?

3. What advice do you have for a manager who has almost no classroom training experience and a big new training assignment? How would you help this manager become effective?

4. Some trainers are more outgoing and sociable with trainees, and some trainers maintain distance from trainees during a program. What is more effective? Are there circumstances that influence or dictate the amount of interpersonal communication between trainers and trainees?

5. Effective trainers typically give and give and give. They give information, they give of themselves, and they give the best training techniques they can find. What do these effective trainers receive in return?

Yearly Career Checkup
Are You in Charge of Your Career?

Today people must manage their own careers. They cannot depend on their organizations to take care of their best interests any more. If you are not managing your career, your work life may be controlling you. Each year around your birthday is good time to evaluate your current job situation. The following assessment is designed to help you be more objective about your current career choices.

Instructions   For each of the following questions answer "yes" (Y) or "no" (N) on the line provided.

_____ 1. On weekends, do you get ideas for improving your effectiveness at work?

_____ 2. Are you as involved in work decisions as you want to be?

_____ 3. When you talk with friends about your work, do you say you only work for the money?

_____ 4. Do you have fantasies about having a different job?

_____ 5. Do you have a good relationship with your boss?

_____ 6. Are you making about the right amount of money for now?

_____ 7. Do you look forward to weekends when you can forget about work?

_____ 8. Do your colleagues care more about your line of work than you do?

_____ 9. Do you have enough decision-making authority over your projects?

_____ 10. Do you see a future for yourself at your organization?

_____ 11. Are you cynical when you talk about the kind of work you do?

_____ 12. Do you fake interest in the work your organization does?

_____ 13. Does your job offer adequate challenges for you to develop new skills?

_____ 14. Do you enjoy the people you work with most of the time?

_____ 15. Are you cynical about performance appraisals from your boss?

_____ 16. Do your friends compliment you on skills and talents you don't use at work?

_____ 17. Are you satisfied with the work environment of your job?

_____ 18. Would you recommend your job to your best friend?

SCORING AND INTERPRETATION

Instructions   Circle the numbers of the items below for which you answered "yes" (Y).

1	2	5	6	9
10	13	14	17	18

If you circled eight or more of the numbers above, it appears you find a lot of satisfaction in your job and you have no compelling reasons to change jobs right now.

Again, circle the numbers of the questions below for which you answered "yes" (Y).

3	4	7	8
11	12	15	16

If you circled six or more of the numbers above, it appears you have a job that is not a good match for your best skills, interests, values, and talents. It may be time to begin considering a job change strategy.

If your responses cannot be easily categorized, look back at the way you answered each individual item. You will find clues about aspects of your job that are not satisfying. You may decide to make some changes in the job you have rather than switch jobs. Take the checkup again at regular intervals to look for indicators of your need to change jobs.

QUESTIONS TO CONSIDER

1. Some people live to work, others work to live. What is your preference? Has it changed over the years? Do you expect your preference to change in the future?

2. Have a conversation with yourself in the mirror. Tell yourself all about your job and your ideas about a great job. After having this conversation, ask yourself what you learned that will help you manage your career successfully. What do you think you will be telling yourself in the future?

3. Managing your own career is not easy. Everything changes. People change, organizations change, the economy changes, and so forth. What changes can you imagine that could impact your work life in the future?

4. The traditional relationship between employer and employee has changed in the past decade. In what ways has this changed your work life? How has it changed work life for members of your family and your friends?

5. Managing your career includes taking responsibility for gathering new information and skills to increase your employability throughout your life. What are three ways you can become involved in this lifelong learning now?

ZzBuzz Words
Do You Understand Buzz Words?

The living, changing language of the work world is buzz words. Complicated ideas are often expressed in only a word or short phrase. Yet buzz words can confuse readers and listeners, too. We forget that other people may not understand what we are saying. (It's even possible we don't understand either.)

Sometimes buzz words are intended to conceal or sugarcoat reality. In that case it can be frustrating to try to figure out the real message. Clear communication demands finding words that are understood by everyone. When that isn't possible, take care to define the terms you use. Check your own understanding by taking the following assessment.

Instructions   Write a clear and brief meaning for the following business terms on the line in front of each one. On the line after the phrase, place a check mark if you have used this term or phrase when speaking and writing.

_____	privatize	_____
_____	a standalone	_____
_____	multicustomer facility	_____
_____	outlease	_____
_____	off-load	_____
_____	paradigm	_____
_____	value-added	_____
_____	skill set	_____
_____	multitasking	_____
_____	outsource	_____
_____	quick fix	_____

_____   reengineered   _____

_____   process improvement   _____

_____   delayering   _____

SCORING AND INTERPRETATION

There are no correct or incorrect answers for this self-assessment. If you wrote meanings for all of the above, check your meanings with other people. Do they agree? Did others in your group have the same ideas? What if most people have an understanding of the term, but one or two people do not know the term?

If you checked that you use most of these terms at work, there is a good chance that people do not truly understand what you mean. This awareness will help you to stop using buzz words unless you are sure everyone understands their meaning. You can substitute other language that people will readily understand. Check by asking people to tell you what they think the buzz words mean.

QUESTIONS TO CONSIDER

1. Think back to your first job. Did you use buzz words? Were they the same or different from the buzz words around you today?

2. Can you think of a metaphor for using buzz words at work? (For example, "Using buzz words at work is like being in another country where you don't know the language.")

3. Some workplaces use more buzz words than others. In your opinion, what workplaces use the most buzz words? Why?

4. What have you done in the past when people used buzz words you did not understand?

5. Did you ever get into a difficult or funny situation because someone used a buzz word that was not clear to everyone else? What happened in this situation?

Part 3

CUSTOMIZING ASSESSMENTS

If you ask experienced trainers whether they have ever customized an existing assessment for a training program, the usual answer is, "Yes, of course."

Trainers are forced to make modifications because, too often, the instruments they find are not the instruments they seek. Customizing is the only way to obtain a better fit for the objectives of a specific training program and a particular group. Trainers develop instruments from scratch, of course, but it takes longer than customizing.

The collection of assessments in this book may be modified for any kind of improvements, small or large, to meet the objectives of a training program. Here are some ways to make modifications, if desired.

- Change a word or phrase.
- Add or delete words and phrases.
- Add or delete items.
- Reorder the items.
- Change the title.

The CD-ROM that accompanies this book makes it simple to make any of the modifications listed above. In addition, clip art, a logo, a border, or other graphic details may be added for a truly customized appearance.

After you have customized your selected assessment, inventory, or questionnaire, the following checklist, which is also available on the CD-ROM, will help you ensure that you have a high-quality instrument.

A Checklist for Customizing

Instructions   Use the checklist below after you have customized an assessment for your own purposes by making a check mark in the box preceding each question if it is true.

☐ Is each item relevant to the training program?
☐ Is each item simple enough for a quick response?
☐ Are the items in the best sequence for your purposes?
☐ Is the reading level appropriate?
☐ Are the items written with everyday, easily understood words?
☐ Are buzz words and jargon appropriate for your respondents?
☐ Are the words for activities used appropriately?

☐ Are the words for jobs and processes used appropriately?

☐ Are the words for people used appropriately (such as *associate* for *employee*)?

☐ Do job titles match those used by participants (such as *manager, supervisor,* or *lead*)?

☐ Are potentially offensive words omitted?

☐ Are unnecessary gender-specific references deleted?

☐ Are unnecessary culture-related items omitted?

☐ Are personally intrusive or revealing items eliminated?

If all of the boxes in the left-hand column are checked, your customized instrument is ready to use for trainees. Any items not marked indicate a need for more work before you can use the customized instrument.

DESIGNING YOUR OWN ASSESSMENTS

If you are unable to find suitable instruments for increasing participant self-awareness and improving workplace performance, you may choose to design your own. Ask yourself the following seven questions to guide you when designing your own questionnaires, instruments, and inventories.

Seven Steps to Success

1. *What do I want trainees to know?* Identify the specific skills, knowledge, behaviors, and attitudes you want trainees to learn about. A useful starting point is to brainstorm a list of as many facts and as much information about your topic as possible. Examine each item on the list for two criteria:

- Is it simple, not complex?
- Is it a single item, rather than two or three items?

2. *What is this instrument intended to measure?* Determine the knowledge base and starting points of your respondents. Be sure you are only assessing one topic with your instrument. It is better to design two targeted instruments than to design one longer, more complex instrument.

3. *How much time do I have to design this instrument?* It may surprise you to discover that it takes one hour to design an instrument or that it takes over five hours. Usually, the more research and background you have on a topic, the faster it is to develop an instrument. However, it is also possible that having too much information can slow down the design process.

When design time is limited, consider using true/false items and rating scales. It takes less time to construct these than it does to construct multiple-choice formats.

4. *How much training time is available for using this instrument?* It takes a certain amount of time to introduce an instrument to participants, answer questions about it, have them complete and score it, and then discuss the experience. Decide the total amount of time available in the overall training design. Be absolutely sure there is sufficient time for discussion after respondents have completed and scored the instrument. A rule of thumb is to plan twice as much time for discussion as for completion of an instrument.

5. *How many items will be included in this instrument?* Determine the actual and ideal amounts of time available for respondents to complete and score the instrument you design. Let this guide the number of items you include on any one assessment. Initially, develop too many items. It is easier to toss out poor items than to find good ones at the last minute.

For a typical brief instrument, plan on using ten to fifteen items. Each item should take respondents approximately thirty seconds to read and answer.

6. *Is there a best way to set up the items?* There are many format choices for an instrument, and most have additional variations. The choices may seem bewildering at first, but surprisingly, once you begin designing an instrument, one or more of the formats will seem an obvious choice given the topic, the time available, or some other factor. The most common format choices include:

- True/false (with variations such as agree/disagree, like/dislike, or yes/no)
- Checklists
- Multiple choice
- Rating scales
- Open-ended statements or questions

Double-check to make sure that each item involves only a single piece of information.

7. *How will I know whether my instrument is good enough?* Ask people you know to take your assessment. Other trainers and workplace acquaintances are good choices. Solicit their frank comments and advice about your instrument. Ask about its usefulness, words and tone, and especially about any area of concern you had when designing the instrument. Consider their comments and advice and make changes to improve your instrument. Also consider asking for feedback from trainees who complete your instrument.

WATCH YOUR WORDS!

All of the instruments in this collection can be customized to maximize their usefulness in training programs. In addition to the customizing tips provided earlier, the following information will help you select the right words and the right tone for your instruments.

This brief guide is designed to increase your awareness and vigilance for the following topics:

- Formal and informal style
- Suitable style for your audience
- Cliches, euphemisms, and jargon
- Gender matters
- Copyrights
- Trademarks

Formal and Informal Style

An assessment, inventory, or questionnaire has a style, much like a personality. It may be formal or informal. This style derives from its format and its language. For most training situations, an informal style is more appropriate because it invites reader participation and involvement.

Look over the descriptions of formal and informal styles below. Use this information to guide you in developing and customizing your own instruments. After you decide to use one style or the other, continue to use it for the entire assessment.

Formal Style

- Tone is impersonal and polite.
- Information is factual and objective.
- Pronouns "you," "I," and "we" are not used.
- No contractions, slang, or humor are used.
- Mostly technical material is covered.
- Sentences are long and complex.
- The passive voice is used.

Informal Style

- Tone is personal and familiar, as though writer and reader are having a conversation.
- Pronouns "you," "I," and "we" are used.
- Thoughts are expressed directly.
- Everyday language is used.
- Contractions, slang, and humor are used.
- Sentences are short and simple.
- Active voice is used.

Suitable Style for Your Audience

Here are six tips for selecting the suitable style for your audience.

1. Use inclusive language as much as possible. Use "we" and "our" and "us" as if speaking to your readers.

2. Use words and phrases that participants understand. For instance, participants in their twenties and participants in their fifties use different slang, and people from various countries around the globe may not understand U.S. slang.

3. Use the active voice. Reword awkward passive voice sentences whenever possible.

4. Use short and direct words so participants focus on self-analysis rather than on the meanings of words. Typically, words at the 8th grade reading level are most suitable.

5. Use simple, everyday words. Write eye glasses, not spectacles; car, not automobile.

6. Write the complete term for acronyms unless you are absolutely sure everyone understands the abbreviated forms.

Cliches, Euphemisms, and Jargon

There is nothing wrong with cliches, euphemisms, jargon, slang, acronyms, and foreign terms. In the right places, they are good choices. For training instruments you create or customize, however, they are probably poor choices.

People with different personal backgrounds, cultural heritages, languages, ideas, and so forth comprise workplaces today. People can be easily confused by one another's familiar ways of expressing themselves. The same words can have different meanings for different people.

To avoid confusion and misunderstandings in customized or newly designed instruments, use only words and terminology that everyone will easily understand. When in doubt, use simple, direct language that is relevant to participants and their workplaces.

Gender Matters

During the past two generations, workplace language has shifted to reflect changes in the workforce, particularly in occupations that were formerly dominated by only men or only women. When creating or customizing training instruments, it is important to select words and phrases that are gender-neutral.

Do you have a gender reference for a Webmaster or programmer? Probably not. These jobs are new and have no gender association for most people. Both men and women started working as Webmasters and programmers at the same time. Workers in most new occupations are as likely to be women as men.

For traditional jobs, it is different. When we refer to a nurse or secretary, we may unthinkingly say "she"—unless we are referring to a specific male worker, whom we may call a "male nurse" or "male secretary." We may incorrectly refer to a fireman, salesman, and mailman as though these workers are male, even when they are female.

Avoid using words that diminish, trivialize, or take away from people, their skills, and their work output. Some words have been in the English language for a long time so, at first, it may seem awkward to change them. When it comes to job titles, avoid describing the worker and focus on the work.

The following additional tips will help you avoid irritating and offending trainees.

- Many English words can be either masculine or feminine, as in "manager," "nurse," and "everyone." Traditionally, masculine pronouns were used to refer to all people. Today, however, it is not considered appropriate to use a masculine pronoun to refer to all people.

- Unless it is absolutely necessary to specify gender, omit it. Usually gender is not relevant. Avoid terms such as authoress, hostess, stewardess, workman, and mailman. Instead use author, host, flight attendant, worker or employee, and mail carrier.

- A woman is not a chairman or a spokesman. When it is awkward to write about a chairperson or spokesperson, it is often most acceptable to call the person a "chair" or a "representative."

- Reword masculine-only phrases such as several "man hours," "the man on the street," and "man the demonstration booth." These could be phrased as "work hours," "the average person on the street," and "staff the demonstration booth."

- Women are adults; avoid referring to them as "girls." Men are adults; avoid referring to them as "boys."

- Write "ladies" only when also writing "gentlemen." Use "women" when also referring to "men." Avoid condescending or patronizing others by using words that convey unequal status of the genders.

- When writing the words "everyone" and "someone," which are singular, you trap yourself into using the difficult he/she/it singular pronouns elsewhere in the sentence. Avoid using "everyone" and "someone" whenever possible.

- "He or she," "him and her," "he/she," "s/he," and "(s)he" can feel artificial for writers and readers. Use them sparingly, if at all. The easiest way to avoid this awkward usage is to rewrite the sentence and change the noun and pronoun to plural form.

- When you choose to use both singular pronouns, help your readers by writing "he or she," "his or her," or "him and her" without slashes, dashes, or parentheses.

- When all the people you write about are of the same gender, use a gender-specific pronoun. For example, "Everyone on the men's team did his best," and "Everyone in the women's group completed her report."

- Avoid gender agreement problems by eliminating pronouns and using articles such as "a," "an," "the," "this," "that," "these," and "those." For example, instead of writing, "Every programmer finished his or her project," write "Every programmer finished a project."

Copyrights

Are you likely to borrow your neighbor's car without permission to run errands—even necessary errands? Probably not. Yet, to create training materials, trainers routinely borrow the creative work of others without permission.

The latest researching and reproducing technologies make it easy to borrow a couple of cartoons, magazine articles, pictures, charts, graphics, music, and film clips—for "educational purposes." Resist the temptation to customize your assessments, inventories, and questionnaires with the creative work of others without obtaining their permission.

Using the work of others without permission, and calling it your own, is illegal. Even when you give full credit, unless you have requested and received specific permission to use the creative work of another person, the law says you cannot use it.

Copyrights give the people who create the registered words and pictures and music a monopoly to control the use of their creations. Materials found on the Internet are covered by the same rules of ownership and usage. To avoid breaking the law, use only material that you create yourself, material that is copyright-free for your use, or material you obtain specific permission to use.

Trademarks

Are you wondering what trademarks have to do with creating and customizing items for training instruments? Answer the following question to determine your trademark savvy.

What do the following short sentences have in common?

- Please pass the kleenex.
- I'll go xerox the report.
- Those are her rollerblades.
- Send the powerpoint to me.

Did you correctly answer that each sentence contains a trademarked word used improperly? Kleenex®, Xerox®, Rollerblade®, and Powerpoint® are trademarked words. The owners of trademarked words and phrases require people using them to follow the rules of trademark usage. Fortunately, the rules are straightforward.

When you use a trademarked word or phrase in a sentence, capitalize the trademarked word or phrase and follow it with its corresponding descriptive noun(s). For example, "Kleenex tissues," "Xerox copies," "Rollerblades skates," and "Powerpoint presentation."

When you use a trademarked word by itself, capitalize it and follow it with a capital R with a circle around it. To correct the examples above, you would write:

- Please pass the Kleenex®.
- I'll go Xerox® the report.
- Those are her Rollerblades®.
- Send the Powerpoint® to me.

Over time, many trademarked words and phrases have become generic: escalator, nylon, realtors, and corn flakes are examples. This happened because the trademark owners were not vigilant about protecting their trademarks. Today, owners of trademarked words do not want their special words to become generic, so they monitor the use of their terms very carefully.

CONCLUSION

This collection of assessments, questionnaires, instruments, and inventories offers a variety of rich resources for trainers and facilitators. To make them immediately useful, the fifty assessments can be photocopied from the book and distributed to trainees. With a little more time to prepare them, the assessments can be imported from the CD-ROM to your favorite word processing program and customized for your training purposes.

The authors want you to be able to use these brief assessments successfully. Part I contained many suggestions for ways to use assessments in group settings and when to use them. Information was also provided about brief self-assessments that could be used to assist novice and experienced trainers alike.

The assessments in Part II were designed to help training participants estimate their own skills, attitudes, knowledge, and behaviors. It rests on the shoulders of a good facilitator to use them and to make participant self-knowledge and self-perception a foundation for new learning and improved performance.

About the Authors

BONNIE BURN has more than twenty years' experience designing and presenting training programs. She has successfully produced customer service, communication, and management skills sessions with a lively, interactive, and results-oriented approach. The La Jolla, California-based consultant first shared her skills in *Flip Chart Power* (Jossey-Bass/Pfeiffer, 1996), a comprehensive book of flip-chart applications. Now she shares some practical tools that have a proven track record with start-up and international organizations, as well as with education and government organizations.

MAGGI PAYMENT is a trainer, facilitator, and principal with the Center for Worktime Options, a San Diego, California, management consulting firm. She specializes in facilitating partnering meetings and developing and implementing flexible workplace and career development programs. With Nancy Stern, she coauthored *101 Stupid Things Trainers Do to Sabotage Success* (Richard Chang Associates, 1995). She has a master's degree in counseling from St. Lawrence University and a bachelor's degree in sociology from Hartwick College. She is an active member of ASTD and Organization Development Network, as well as an avid reader and reviewer of business books.